Defining Moments

For Therapists

Edited by
Serge Prengel
& Lynn Somerstein

LifeSherpa

Published by LifeSherpa, an imprint of Proactive Change®, New York, NY

Library of Congress Control Number: 2013935235

ISBN: 978-1-892482-25-9

I would like to dedicate this book to the Integral Yoga Institute and to the Institute for Expressive Analysis.

Lynn Somerstein

This book is also dedicated to the modern media that allow us to share our experiences. Please join us:

- on Linked In: http://linkedin.integrativeprocess.com
- on facebook: http://fb-dmft.lifesherpa.com

Serge Prengel

Contents

The 10 drawings between chapters are by Robin Kappy, who also wrote a chapter, Room to Grow.

The drawing that follows Marianne Gunther's story is by her.

The cover art is by Cathy Marie Begg.

All cases discussed in these chapters are composites as opposed to representing an actual person.

Introduction

Lynn Somerstein

Psychotherapy is about change. Clients come to therapy seeking change and a better life, and, in the process the therapist changes too. The book *Defining Moments* shows how therapists transform and grow in response to their private life experiences and to the relationship they and their clients develop together. Therapy is a relational two way street; there are many stops along the way, and not always what we expect.

A couple of years ago I was telling Serge how my roles as psychoanalyst and yoga teacher, which I had deliberately held separate, began to integrate. One day I saw that the best way to get through to a particular person was with a body oriented technique, a yoga asana, and I asked her to stand in mountain pose. This is an everyday yoga asana, but it is not standard psychotherapy practice, so I thought a long time before I made the suggestion. I was also a little worried that the psychoanalytic police, the cops who live in my head, would tell me that a "real" psychoanalyst would never do such a thing. I felt pretty daring at the time, but in truth therapists are always trying to figure out the best ways to help people.

Sometimes what we think works best is different than what we are trained to do, and even feels like a transgression, but my professional reorganization was central to my being and reflected my life's values. I was on firm ground too, a graduate of two esteemed institutes, one for yoga, and one for psychoanalysis.

Serge and I began talking about the *integrative* approach to psychotherapy, which holds that each of the many kinds of therapy hold their own truth and reflect a part of our glorious human diversity; he suggested gathering all kinds of experiences in which therapists face events that lead to the redefinition of identity and process. The goal of a project began to emerge -- we would capture the therapist's evolving sense of self. Serge suggested asking interested colleagues to contribute chapters to the book that came to be called *Defining Moments*. These chapters include examples of psychoanalysis, psychotherapy, body therapy, art therapy, and pre and perinatal psychology, among others.

The results are moving, haunting sometimes. Every person wrote about something different, from perinatal experience to dying, and in between child abuse, rape and murder. The therapists were often afraid that they might have transgressed; at least they went beyond the usual boundaries, some working with lucid dreaming, others touching the client, one person giving a gift. Another therapist used the musical themes that went through her head as clues to her client's needs. One therapist describes wanting more in her own life. A particularly touching chapter shows the chemistry between the therapist and her client.

If you've been curious about some of the things therapists experience doing treatment and how they got to be therapists in the first place, here's your chance to find out.

The Music of Awakening

Merle Molofsky

Many years ago I began supervising a talented analytic candidate, who had just begun clinical work. She was a singer, and, as such, was very immersed in the power of song, the synergy of music and words. She was readily empathic and attuned with the people she had begun to work with, and then found herself baffled when she felt out of touch with a man with whom she had met with for only a few sessions. As we talked about her most recent session with him, and her feelings about him, and her understanding of him – or, rather, her sense that she was failing to understand him – I had an "aha" moment that led to her own "aha". Knowing that she was a singer, and seeing that all our talk was going nowhere, I said, "Is he a song? Can you sing a song that is who he is?" And she immediately began singing, "Sometimes I feel like a motherless child, a long way from home".

As I type these words, I find myself feeling a chill, a trembling chill in my lungs, just as I did those many years ago when first she sang the song that was the man she learned she did understand. According to

Chinese medicine, the lungs are the seat of grief, sadness, numbness, and depression. The words of the song, "Sometimes I Feel Like a Motherless Child", readily convey grief and sorrow, a longing and loneliness that could lead to depression. The slow, meandering melody underscores those feelings. The woman I supervised realized that superficially, she was seeing a man who was very macho, big, blustery, even slightly scary. But the song helped her realize she was seeing a scared, lonely, abandoned child, a "motherless child".

The Source

Music speaks to me in many ways. There is one way in particular that evolved early in my life, a way that has helped to create resonance. My parents were verbally communicative. We were poor. They were working class, with limited formal education, but with far-reaching intellectual ability, far-reaching curiosity, so that they were highly cultured, self-educated people, eager to share with their two children the riches of literature, history, art, music, and more. They were affectionate and kind. And, like so many people of their background and generation, shy about emotional self-expression.

They talked to me about themselves in music, without quite knowing how much they were saying. And I, without realizing what I was attuning to, resonated with their musical communication. My father had a sweet voice, and knew three or four chords on the guitar. He sang mostly folk songs, and a few pop songs. My mother was inhibited in many ways, and was reluctant to sing. When she sang, her voice quavered, and sometimes she had trouble staying on pitch. Despite her inhibition, she sang lullabies, and stayed on pitch. The lullabies she sang were mainly Yiddish lullabies, and a few English language ones as well.

My mother came from a highly traumatic background. She was born in Poland, to a very poor Orthodox Jewish family, and emigrated here in 1920, when she was 10 years old. She was the first-born child, and her three younger brothers starved to death during World War I. In America, two more children were born, her mother became very ill, and when my mother was 13, her mother was hospitalized, her siblings were put in foster care, and she left school to work as a domestic.

When she sang lullabies to me in Yiddish, what was I resonating with in her? I felt her yearning, her sorrow, her hope and delight. I didn't learn about her life story until I was 10 years old, the same age she was when she came to America. But I learned her life story in feelings, heart-strings to heart-strings, as she sang. I heard her mother singing to my mother's baby brothers, I heard my mother comforting her baby brothers by singing to them as well. I heard her singing to the two babies born here. I heard her grief at the death of the babies who died in Poland, I heard her grief at losing, temporarily, the two babies born here.   I heard her missing her own mother, remembering her mother singing.   And I heard her grateful that her own two children, born here, in the safety of American poverty, would have enough to eat, and would grow up remembering they were Jewish and would grow up American.

To have heard all that, without knowing what I was learning, has made me resonant with sound – the sound of a person's voice. I hear the depth of feeling before I know the story that will evolve.

Story. I never learned Yiddish. But I learned the sound of Yiddish, and the rich culture conveyed in the tonality of Yiddish.   When I was six years old, my mother taught me to read Yiddish, even though I didn't understand Yiddish.   Once I could read, she opened a book of stories by I. L. Peretz, written in Yiddish, and asked me to read a story out loud. As I read, she translated into English.   The story was "Bontche Schweig", "Bontche the Silent". Overtly, the story taught me something about my mother's heritage and values. The unconscious teaching I resonated with was my mother's own silence.

Story: Bontche was a child of extreme poverty and deprivation, fending for himself through trials and tribulations from a very early age. When he died, his soul in heaven was examined, as all souls were, and he was found to be truly saintly, because he never uttered a word of complaint, never reproached God, lived each day in appreciation of the gift of life. Hence Bontche

Schweig, Bontche the Silent. Silent in the face of all earthly suffering. The angels sang his praises, and he looked around for the great soul they were honoring, not realizing they were honoring him. He then was told that now, since he was in heaven, he could have anything he wanted. Anything, he wondered. Anything.

What did Bontche ask for? He asked, so humbly, could he please have a warm roll every morning – with a little bit of butter. And all the angels, and God himself, wept.

The message I learned was the message in the Passover Seder, the message of "dayenu" – "it would be sufficient" -- that anything God did for the escaping Israelites would have been sufficient. I learned my mother's gratitude for finding what she had found when she fled the deaths of her brothers in Poland and, later, trusted in the sufficiency that her children in America would live. And that if we heard the tonality of the sound of Yiddish, the sound of Yiddish lullabies, something that had died in Poland would live in *di Goldene Medina*, the Golden Land, America.

I attuned to the sound of a voice, to the cadences of a language I did not speak, and learned in my heart all I could not formulate into words, into story, until I was much older, and heard the words, the story. I heard more than words and story, though. I learned feeling.

Returning From Then To Do More Now

Therefore, I have learned that sometimes an "aha" moment during an analytic session comes through an associative process that is not immediately perceived as verbal. My experience in session with evenly hovering attention, with reverie, with what Bion recommends as listening without memory or desire or understanding, leads me to "hear" melodies when I am in session. When I "hear" melodies, I remember lyrics.

For instance, I might hear a fragment of an American ballad, "I am a man of constant sorrow, I've seen trouble all my days," when someone I'm working with is talking in a rather brittle fashion about this and that, chitchat about his day at work, or a TV show. The song fragment alerts me to an underlying emotion that the chit-chatter is trying to suppress. "Aha." Now I realize.... and as I ask a question or two, the feeling emerges.

Or, a woman I'm working with is complaining bitterly about "men". How "men" are shallow, unpredictable, untrustworthy. Have the men she has dated been so shallow, et cetera? No, she replies, she wouldn't get that close with anyone, all her dates are variants of "speed dating", one or two dates and then she cuts bait, she bails. And then a melody, a song fragment, arises – an American ballad, as sung by Joan Baez. "Don't sing love songs, you'll wake my mother, she's lying here, right by my side, and, in her hand, a silver dagger, she says that I can't be your bride." Further lyrics lead me further along on the "aha" trail.

"All men are false, says my mother, they'll tell you wicked, loving lies, the very next evening they'll court another, leave you alone to pine and sigh. My daddy is a handsome devil, he has a chain five miles long. And on every link a heart does dangle, of some poor maid he's loved and wronged." Aha. I realize I have to ask about her mother, her father, their relationship, her feelings about both of them.

In another instance, I might hear a snippet from a movie, "Night on Earth", in which Wynona Rider says, "Men! Can't live with them, can't live without them, can't shoot them, men!" And the movie snippet leads to the country and western song by the Forester Sisters, "Men". Which itself is a variant on a theme, as the original quote is by Erasmus, "Women, can't live with them, can't live without them". The person I am working with may not have been saying anything in the moment that evokes the despair of the "battle of the sexes", but if I "hear" that quote as part of my associative process, and then the song, sure enough, eventually the lament, in one form or another, shortly follows.

In working with a couple, when the wife complained about not receiving enough physical affection, and the husband grew restive and surly, I associated to an Aretha Franklin song, "hearing" the melody, and then I associated to a Shangri-La's song, again, "hearing" the melody. First came the melodies, then the words. The Aretha Franklin song was "Natural Woman". The Shangri-La's song was "Give

Him a Great Big Kiss". When I paid attention to the seemingly distracting fragments of melody, I "tuned in" to the words. Of course, the wife wanted physical affection, and my association led me to the realization that the husband needed to understand that indeed he had to make her "feel like a natural woman". Similarly, the husband felt chastised and criticized, and my association led me to realize that the wife needed to realize that her complaints sounded like parental attacks to the husband, and that while she pleaded for love, he heard "Yeah, well I hear that he's bad". The lyric, however, completes the line with "Mmm, he's good bad, but he's not evil".

The "aha" reverberated further. The next session, I brought two CDs with me to my office, and played the two songs for the couple. I offered them a language in which they could understand each other, a code they could use that would communicate their emotional experience. She could ask for love by singing a line or two of "Natural Woman", and he could ask for reassurance that she loved and valued him and didn't think he was hopelessly unforgivable by singing a line or two of "Give Him a Great Big Kiss". The music itself augments the words. Aha, music intensifies emotion! Aha, this is not an epiphanic discovery, we've always known that! Aha, yes it is, it is ephiphanic every time we use the intensity of word and music combined to communicate more deeply than we might have with words alone.

We all have the capacity to live in an ongoing unfolding series of epiphanic moments. Our free associative processes are with us ever and anon, we perceive them, sometimes consciously, sometimes unconsciously. "Aha!" is the recognition that we reverberate with each other, and with the world. That "resonance', that "reverberation", underlies the philosophy embodied in "music of the spheres", "Musica Universalis", that the entire cosmos is proportioned mathematically, that the energies of the universe are mathematical, and have musical properties, are expressed musically. "As above, so below", attributed to Hermes Trismegistus, is an element in many philosophies. Our mind-bodies are tuning forks, attuned to the universe. Let's listen to each other.

Merle Molofsky is a psychoanalyst in private practice in New York City, a published poet, and a produced playwright. She serves on the Board of Directors, International Forum for Psychoanalytic Education; Board of Advisors and as faculty and supervisor, Harlem Family Institute; and as faculty member and supervisor, National Psychological Association for Psychoanalysis. She is on the Editorial Board of The Psychoanalytic Review, *and from 2010-2012 served as Editor of the on-line psychoanalytic and creative arts journal* Other/Wise. *In 2012, the National Association for the Advancement for Psychoanalysis gave her their annual Gradiva Award for Poetry. Her play, "Koolaid", was produced at Lincoln Center. Her poetry books include:* Ladder of Words, *and* Mad Crazy Love: Love Songs and Mad Poems, *Poets Union Press, 2011. Other publications include a chapter in* Many Paths, One Journey, *and articles in psychoanalytic journals.*

Defining Moments Between Boundaries and Within Space

Mary J. Giuffra

My life has been a search for the right sized space, big enough to safely experience overwhelming emotions, such as deep sorrow or raging anger, and small enough so I can support others and their feelings, so they can feel safe too. . Right now I feel constricted, the aftermath of trauma and the lack of physical mobility. Vast uncontained space and too tight boundaries are equally overwhelming.

To begin this paper I selected moments with clients that felt related to space. In each of the four defining client moments, boundaries were needed to contain space. Yet, several months ago a traumatic event occurred in my personal life that expanded this perception. Currently, I am in the middle of a personal defining moment in which space feels constricted while the aftermath of trauma and a lack of physical mobility restrict available space. As some find the vastness of uncontained space overwhelming, I am experiencing the constraint of boundaries.

Breaking through boundaries in a gracious way is the essence of growth. While change implies a death of the old and birth of the new, it can also be a genuine expansion or transformation. A breakthrough in or of space does not have to be about severing ties. Rather it can be about transforming while maintaining connection. Four defining moments in my career have helped me to experience this rhythmic and gracious or choppy and awkward dance of growth between space and boundaries. I believe therapists are like dance coaches who help clients navigate the spacious dance of life.

I began my professional career as a labor and delivery nurse, welcoming and occasionally guiding little ones into this life space; breaking through boundaries in a gracious way is the essence of growth, transforming while maintaining connection. This is often, but not always, a glorious experience.

Once, when I was working as a nurse in the maternity ward, I met a young couple named Lucy and Michael. They had deeply longed for a baby, but their baby was stillborn, he never found the right space to breathe in this vast life force. I couldn't help the baby; how could I help Lucy and Michael? I felt so helpless. How could I ease their pain?

Some family members and staff cautioned against the parents seeing their limp little one, but Lucy and Michael wanted to hold their still baby, so I dressed him in a tiny hospital- issued blue and white striped knit cap, and wrapped him in a tiny shirt and fluffy receiving blanket, which I hoped would soften their shock and grief when they held him. I asked them what the baby's name was, and affirmed them in their decision to hold little Michael Jr. and say goodbye to him. We hugged one another and cried together, and I knew then that I needed to learn a lot more about helping people recover from tragedy, and I decided to study and become a psychotherapist.

I began my studies of trauma, and learned the biology behind hugs and tears. Trauma shuts down the dorsal vagal nervous system, activating the fight or flight response; shared hugs and tears cause the ventral vagal nervous systems to come back on line, enabling people to become socially engaged, an attachment response. I understood how our shared tears and hugs had helped Lucy and Michel endure the tragedy of their baby's death.

Sharing those hugs and tears helped me too. I continued my studies and opened my private practice as a therapist.

One of my early experiences as a therapist was very frightening. At the behest of a school guidance counselor a family, Rose and Sam, and their daughter Jane, came to me for therapy. Sam was not happy to be sitting in my office and rolled his eyes disgustedly whenever his wife spoke. I noted that and asked Rose what she was feeling. Rose looked down at the floor and whispered, "I'm worried about Jane." "And your greatest fear?" At this point Sam, a powerful tall man, lifted his foot and crossed it over his knee. From my peripheral vision, I noticed a small object peeking out from his sock. It looked like a very small Dick Tracy toy gun with a pearl handle. "What is that in your sock," I asked. Sam looked me straight in the eye, "A gun." "I don't like guns and prohibit them in my office. Please leave the gun in your car, Sam." He got up and returned without the gun. Rose looked up in horror as she saw me establish a boundary for my professional space. The therapist must create a safe space; no one can do this work feeling afraid. It was a defining moment for me because I knew that no matter what theory I was applying, I did not allow guns in the office and that was my bottom line and I held it.

As the space keeper and self-appointed boundary maker Sam previously refused to tolerate his wife or daughter establishing boundaries without his approval. Sam used subtle or not so subtle threats to intimidate Rose and Jane and he attempted to intimidate me. However I was clear that this was my professional space and I designed the boundary to give clients a safe space. This was also a defining moment for Jane as she looked up with admiration and the barest hint of a smile when her father returned to the office without his weapon.

Another defining moment occurred during a session in which I invited fifteen year old Athena's parents to attend our session. After an initial family session with her parents, I saw Athena alone for several months. She was delightful. Athena wore heavy boots, rings in her nose and ears, tri-colored hair and listened to her brand of Goth music. In general Goth music focuses on topics parents and our culture tend to ignore, such as racism and other social evils. Teens are creating boundaries to define their personal as well as communal space. Once I learned that Athena was in a Goth group with wonderful if different values, I was relieved and fascinated. It was a true education for me. She educated me about the different types of Goth clothing, behavior, music, boots, literature and philosophy. Some Goths were good and loving. Others were not. Some Goths were optimistic and saw beauty in the world while others were more solemn and tried to find the meaning in life, death and suffering.

I understood that clothes can define teenagers (adults as well) Preppy, Hippie, Goth, cool depending on the context. I forgot to tell you Athena's parents looked as if they stepped out of a Ralph Lauren catalogue. Athena was making a statement- she was different, not like her parents.

During the session with her parents, Athena's mother started a barrage of criticism and enlisted her husband to tell Athena how unhappy they were with their daughter and her Goth friends. Athena got up and left the office. At the time, I didn't know about the fight/flight response in therapy but Athena was fleeing to a safer space. Of course, I second-guessed myself thinking perhaps I should have intervened sooner. Still, I sensed that Athena was seeking some calm inner space. While she was gone, I held a large enough space to contain her parents, their frustration and their deep love for Athena. I also explained Athena's need for personal boundaries. Her parents softened when I asked them about their teen years during the late sixties. They smiled and remembered how hard it was to be a teen. Almost as if on cue, Athena returned to the room, looked at her parents and said, "I accept you, why can't you accept me?" It was a spiritual moment in which the container expanded sufficiently so each member of the family could take enough space to be who they are and experience one another's boundary.

How can you, therapist and client, experience anger and be safe? When I was a peer counselor in an addictions training program a member of my group began pounding a bataka or stuffed bat on a pillow while she kneeled on the floor. Following the most furious frenzy of anger I had ever witnessed, this young woman got up from the floor looking stoned, perhaps frozen would be a better word. I was trained in a cathartic modality; I knew that grounding the client was a precursor to anger work. Yet, I was always leery that in spite of grounding, cathartic anger work might not be effective, it was like piercing a boil to drain it without ever getting to the root of the infection. The issue remained unresolved and the intensity of reactivity grew. This was a defining moment and led me to Somatic Experiencing, a therapeutic modality that teaches the importance of containing anger in the body and releasing it in a titrated manner so that you can experience the anger on a deep and profound physiologic level and release the unexpressed physiologic response in a contained manner rather than reactively dumping it into your environment. In Somatic Experiencing, the space for the work is both defined and elastic. I am pleased to say that research has supported my belief that cathartic anger work is not an effective technique for growth and boundary setting (Bushman, 2001).

As I mentioned in the opening paragraph this is an interesting time for me as I am currently experiencing boundary constriction and what feels like a restriction of personal space. Of course, this is an ideal opportunity to go deeper into inner space but that's not my focus right now. I am in the middle of a personal defining moment. On a recent trip to Russia and the Balkans my husband was mugged and suffered a fractured hip, clavicle and head wounds. He was in four hospitals in three different countries including Sweden where he had surgery on his hip. Because Swedish hospitals are quiet and Zen-like, our time there allowed for peaceful inner space. In contrast, New York hospitals evoked piercing loudspeaker announcements, blaring televisions and earsplitting carts rolling down the corridors. In Sweden, the carts were fitted with large silent rubber wheels.

Before entering the space of a patient's room in Sweden, doctors, nurses, cleaning staff and therapists of every ilk knocked on my husband's door and waited for a response before entering. They were respectful of his personal space and ours. My son flew to Sweden from New York and my daughter from Paris. Family space collapsed to support one another. At home, their sister dealt with insurance companies and rehabilitation hospitals while their older brother sought contacts to expedite the process. The challenge of the trauma mobilized family space to heal my husband and their father.

Our space was greatly expanded in Latvia when the acting ambassador from the American Embassy called our hotel (my daughter in New York had informed the Embassy) to tell me she would be at the hotel at nine in the morning to accompany me to the Latvian hospital where my husband was taken by ambulance. I was relieved as I had left the hospital at 2:00 AM that morning feeling overwhelmed, particularly since I spoke no Latvian and the police had not arrived for seven hours. The ambassador and her assistant spent the day at the hospital and explained that the purpose of the American Embassy is to support Americans who are abroad. The boundaries to contain our trauma were expanding to include our country. An Embassy staff person returned the following day and remained with us until the SAS ambulance plane arrived to take us to Stockholm for the surgery. My son was at the Stockholm airport when the plane landed. Our daughter arrived from France two days later exclaiming that her pilot announced Sweden is a noise free airport. Boundaries forbid loud speakers from booming out flight and gate numbers. Peaceful space prevails.

After a calm two weeks at Danderyds Sjukhus in Stockholm, our insurance company sent a flight nurse to Sweden to accompany my husband and me for our return to NYU/Rusk Rehabilitation Hospital. He created a safe space for our flight home to New York. We began to leave the Zen-like reverie of Sweden as the loud sounds at JFK pierced our ears. No boundaries forbade loud noises in this airport. After eighteen days at Rusk and three weeks in sub-acute care my husband returned home to continue his rehabilitation and my boundaries began to contract. He needed assistance in walking up and down stairs-- home health care provided physical and occupational therapy and nursing care, but I needed to be at home.

Planned conferences were canceled, workshops postponed till next year, our spontaneous dinners out, all the things we loved doing together stopped. Of necessity, boundaries were tightened and communal space constricted. I had a sense of what it must be like for people who get older and retire from careers. It is truly a defining moment and we are in the throes of it. Now that the electrician has illumined our home with lights that go on as soon as you pass them and the plumber has installed bars to hold as my husband bathes in the shower, our home space is becoming safer for my husband who has graduated from a walker to a cane. Our home is now a secure container for older folks as well as children. We are on a journey and in the middle of a very defining moment in our lives. It feels calmer and less frenetic than our previous life but our freedom is different. I am curious to see where this defining moment will lead. It is fun to spend so much time together but strange to have my husband ask me where I am going. The dance of boundaries and space continues but I am the dancer and not the coach. I hope to do it graciously.

Book quoted:

Bushman, Brad J. Does venting anger feed or extinguish the flame? Catharsis, Rumination, Distraction, Anger and Aggressive Responding. Personality and Social Psychology Bulletin, 9/2001, pp 724-731

Mary J. Giuffra, Ph.D., has been a therapist for over 30 years during which time she has worked with individuals, families, and couples using a unique blend of body-mind techniques. Dr. Giuffra received her doctorate from New York University and is a New York State Licensed Marriage and Family Therapist, a Board Certified Clinical Specialist in Psychiatric Mental Health, and a New York State Registered Professional Nurse. Dr. Giuffra has also been recognized for her pioneering efforts as an educator and specialist in curriculum development. She has served as a tenured member of the faculty at New York University and the College of Mount Saint Vincent. Dr. Giuffra has been the recipient of several major grants from the federal government and is the author of countless articles in peer reviewed journals, and book chapters.

Soul Geisha

Linda Marks

Things of quality have no fear of time, and as I reflect and write about the defining moments that led me to be a body psychotherapist, I see threads of meaning and layers of experience slowly emerge in the crucible of time.

There are two parts to my story. The first, what I call "the original story," are the lessons that have informed the body psychotherapy method I have developed, taught and practiced for the past 27 years. I think of this as choosing life, following my heart. The second story, which is newer, looks at deeper and more personal revelations that reach far beyond my professional practice, and explores how the defining moment not only led to my path of work as a body psychotherapist, but also deeply shaped my experience as a human being and woman. I have come to realize the impact was so deep, it feels as though the defining moment shaped my DNA.

As a very small child, I knew deep down inside that I was here on this earth to make a profound difference. In spite of being a shy, introverted child, I was recognized as a natural leader-I identified with John F. Kennedy and Martin Luther King. JFK, MLK and Robert Kennedy were all assassinated in what seemed to be a heartbeat, when I was a barely school-aged child. I said to God, "I am afraid to commit to my life mission, because if I am like MLK, JFK and Robert Kennedy, I might be shot."

I felt a tightness in my chest and a knot in my stomach. I asked myself how was I going to take my place in this world?

I led in spite of myself. I was elected and selected to take on more positions of leadership. I became a pioneer anorexic at age 13. Fighting a battle within myself to be "perfect," to be "good enough, I found myself learning the hard way that if I let my mind control my body, I could end up dead. I tried hard to be a "perfect" child, but no matter how much I accomplished, nothing was ever good enough for my judgmental, critical parents, so, I willed myself to model thinness, lost my period for 9 months at age 13, and found myself walking the thin line between life and death.

I was in spiritual, emotional and psychic anguish. But my heart's pain was invisible to those around me, who only saw me as an amazing leader, someone who could leap over obstacles in a single bound. I felt alone and so different from everyone else. Was I?

Everything changed one August night, the summer I was 16 years old. I worked at Fenway Park, Boston's baseball stadium, and took public transportation home. While I was afraid of the rowdy drunks and punks near the ballpark, I discovered my greatest danger was closer to home, right behind the Brigham's Ice Cream shop where I had my second job. As I walked by the alley in back of the Brigham's on my way home to my parents' house, a stranger came out of the shadows, reached out from behind me, grabbed hold of my leather pocketbook strap, and proceeded to carefully wrap it around my neck before knocking me down to the ground.

Like an audience member watching a play, I felt myself detach from the gruesome plot, but this was not a play. It was my life.

The man, who was about 6'2", quickly showed me that even my strong 5'7" frame could easily be captured and bound—both by his anger and energy and by my own paralyzing fear. My body became a numb fortress as I tried to keep his penetration actions out, and my fear in.

My mind started racing, but I took a few deep breaths to slow myself down, to get grounded and find whatever well of inner wisdom I might have that could keep me alive. At first I tried to fight him off, but he was bigger than me and very angry. I quickly discovered how easily a raging man could overpower a frightened 16 year old girl.

I tried to talk my way out by telling him the penalty for statutory rape (I had taken a class called "The Law and the Individual.") and offering to get him another girl if he let go. Bargaining and chatting only pissed him off and his grip grew stronger around my neck. He tried to strangle me and I used every bit of the diaphragmatic breathing I had learned as a singer to keep myself alive. I was close to the edge of life; I knew if he pushed much harder, I would I would fall off.

Suddenly he gave up in exasperation. He couldn't kill me. He decided instead that since I would not die, he would drag me into the nearby alley and rape me, repeating "Why did I pick you lady? Why did I pick you?"

Once in the alley, I asked him to take the pocketbook strap off my neck, which he used to control me by strangling me, and he said, "No. That is my security belt." My body sprang into intuitive hyperdrive, recognizing that if I didn't tune in more deeply and move to a place beyond anything I knew, I was not going to come out of this experience alive. Within my heart, I recognized the fear of my own mission that had been haunting me, that if I committed myself fully to my path, the deep one that I knew from inside, a stranger would kill me just like JFK or Martin Luther King had been killed. I was only 16, and that stranger had already come out of the shadows; my life was already on the line.

A little voice inside my heart said to turn it over to the God I was not raised to believe in. Without thinking, I opened up my heart and said to God, "I want to live!" A little voice answered back, "Then you need to commit to your mission." Without thinking, once again, I spoke from my heart and said to God, "I commit."

A voice then came from within my heart that said to forgive the man who was trying to beat me and rape me. Without waiting a heartbeat, I opened my mouth and spoke from my heart, and said, "I forgive you" to the man.

He stopped in his tracks and burst into tears. "I don't want to be doing this," was his first reply. As I lay on my back, half frozen and half relieved, I held the space for this man to empty out his anguished soul.

He had been in jail before. He had raped and murdered other women. He said if they ever caught him and put him back in jail, he would take a gun to his head and kill himself. He cried and cried and purged himself of his shame, fear, and rage; I solidly and faithfully held the space, part stone and part sacred intimate, transforming myself from a crime statistic to a therapist in the birth canal; this murderer and rapist was my first client.

Though my presence gave him the space to cry and sob, I was frightened. How was I going to save my own life? The man began to feel his exposure and started to gather in his anger to "pull himself back together," and a knot in my stomach started to form as I realized that I was out of things I could say or do.

In the blink of an eye, as I lay there, frozen on my back, praying that God would find a way to keep me alive, because NOW, I really DID want to live—more deeply than I ever had before. I opened my heart. I prayed in whatever way I felt I could pray. Suddenly a car came down the alley, and the man grabbed his pants and ran off. I was so frozen; I could not tell if I was relieved or just going through the motions of responding to what had happened, like a news reporter on TV.

The driver saw me, a teenage girl, laying naked in the alley on a bed of rocks, and stopped to help. I reached for my high school tennis jacket, stood up, still barely there, and knocked on the car window. I asked the driver to take me home, and I could feel his compassion radiate through the windows. "The same thing happened to my wife when she was your age," he said.

As I got into his car, I realized I had just experienced something huge. It was more to process than I could put my hands or arms around at that moment. But, metaphorically, I recognized that by following my heart and turning it over to a higher power which I had touched within my own soul, I had chosen my life, and had my prayers answered.

One can say this was the defining moment when God made me aware I was a therapist. And my path in this world was a path of heart. By listening to my heart, by following my heart, by speaking from my heart, by speaking to the heart, I was alive and NOT just a crime statistic. And though much of the psychic healing and the PTSD that ensued took years, if not decades to embrace, integrate and understand, some very deep part of me, in my heart, my solar plexus and my core KNEW that this was a turning point in my life.

When I said, "I forgive you," the man burst into tears and stopped beating me. Metaphorically, he was my first therapy client. And reaching from my heart to the depths of his heart saved my life, and transformed me from a potential crime statistic to a sacred intimate/healer. In time, I realized that what saved my life was the power of the heart, and that by listening to my heart, first I chose my life, and later, I chose to treasure and savor the gift of life and help others do the same. I now recognized first-hand what a precious gift life is.

I found myself referring back to this experience again and again and again as I both followed my personal healing journey, and found myself in spaces to work with others who came to heal from trauma by embracing the power of the heart. In time, I realized that the information in our body, and especially in our hearts, is a natural inner guidance system. By learning to create emotional safety within myself, including breathing, slowing down, being in the moment and making room for my heart's voice to speak and be heard, I was tapping into deeper wisdom within myself and even beyond myself. I saw that my heart really was interconnected with a larger consciousness, a larger heart, and that the larger heart was always there for me to tap into, and to teach others to tap into as well.

Over the years, as I both worked to help myself heal fully from this trauma, and learned to create a deeper and deeper emotional space that could hold others in their joy and in their pain, I came to realize that what initially felt like a horrible experience had actually become a gift.

I learned very literally about the power of the heart, and the power of my own heart. And I learned that when we really need something, the universe does provide. I learned how important it is to listen deeply, both to my own heart and to the heart of others, including those, like the man who attacked me, who I might think was not the man to bring into my heart. I learned to trust the subtle sensations in my body, including the intuitive sense of knowing, in both my body and my heart, and to follow the guidance my body sensations provide.

There were many lessons from the heart, but two of the most important ones were embracing life as a precious gift to be treasured every single day, and the privilege it is to become what I call a "soul geisha" — someone who holds a space that honors the other person's heart and soul, whoever they are, however deep their pain. My internal sensing system was calibrated that day, and over the years has been tuned and refined to serve me in my work with clients and in life.

Hard to believe that looking back, in my heart, I feel this turning point was actually more of a blessing or gift. Had it not happened, I might never have found a right way to really LIVE. Love, indeed, is an alternative life style!

My experience with the man in the alley opened a pathway to my mission as "therapist or soul geisha, a sacred intimate," where in order to hold a space of profound healing, my human needs and vulnerabilities were compartmentalized and removed from the sacred space I held first for the man who tried to kill me, and later, for all who came to me in search of healing. Over time I have come to realize, my experience of "therapist as soul geisha" or "sacred intimate," permeated my DNA much more deeply than just as a professional frame of reference. My experience lying on my back in the pebbled alley, surrendering to God, embracing my mission and becoming a vessel for healing became a template for all of my life—both inside and outside of my therapy office.

It is as if my soul's DNA was restructured without an on and off button. I could not selectively choose to put my humanness, including my human needs and womanhood, aside in service of my client's highest good, and restore my full humanity when I stepped outside of the office. The experience felt much like what a man might feel like when he tries to take his armor off after many days in the battlefield. Even if he makes the effort and goes through the physical motions, the emotional part of the armor may not so easily peel off. Instead, the self-less, spiritually informed sacred healing environment carried over into my personal life. With all the work therapists do to avoid their countertransference contaminating the therapeutic container, I realize I had the opposite experience. The self-containment I brought to create a space of sacred healing infiltrated my personal life.

In the role of therapist, I embraced the hero's journey, offering a divine and profound healing gift. However, in doing so, the cost to my personhood was not heroic at all, but was actually tragic.   After the attempted rape and murder, outside of the therapy office, I ceased living the hero's journey. Instead, I became a tragic protagonist trapped in a web set by the Gods.   This happened without my conscious awareness or consent.

Some therapists feel impelled to act as a therapist to their families and their friends. I, for one, have been very clear that I will not be therapist to my friends and loved ones, because I treasure the equal, mutual, peer, two-way sharing and vulnerability of that kind of relationship.

Many therapists and healers become the vessel in service of their clients. But it is critical that there be a boundary between the person who is the healer and the space of sacred intimate they create to help others heal. Finding a way to both be a healing vessel and also a human being and woman has been an unexpected, challenging and often painful path that has unfolded since the attempted rape and murder I experienced at age 16.

I went from being overpowered to finding power in helping others. I have been working for many years to restore my personal power and my power as a woman, which includes the power to be vulnerable and surrender, and be safe and taken care of when I am vulnerable and surrendered. In my personal life, my sacred intimate energy has attracted men who recognize that connecting with me can fill their emotional and psychic wells. However, often this is without recognition by the other that this kind of sacred gift really needs to be a two way street.

I had not agreed to become "a cosmic tit," a paradise for male souls to feast without conscience, and sometimes take without recognizing their responsibility for giving back and doing their own deeper work. I spend a lot of time covering other people's backs, and sometimes I yearn to have someone cover my back. Others derive great connection from my bounty, but when my own connection needs are not factored into the equation I feel isolated.

This has not been an act of martyrdom. And truthfully, I don't see any psychic payback for being a 24-7 sacred intimate in life. The experience feels as though it lives in the transgenerational energy field that is accessed in Family Constellations work.

Children seldom or never dare to live a happier or more fulfilling life than their parents. Unconsciously they remain loyal to unspoken family traditions that work invisibly. Family Constellations are a way of discovering underlying family bonds and forces that have been carried unconsciously over several generations. -Bertold Ulsamer

I am just not sure if my experience is transgenerational or more fundamentally transpersonal. It has been very clear that what has transpired in my relationships is beyond the psychological and interpersonal levels.

Rape is a travesty of love. On the one hand, the rapist "wants you," but not for who you are at a soul deep level. In rape there is desire, but not for the person you are. It's the desire for what you can provide, a desire filled by an object. It is so impersonal it is the opposite of being loved for who you are.

While, on the one hand, I had the gift of not being killed in the moment, and the gift of being able to continue on in my life, I also feel like I have been carrying a heavy cross of sorts. This cross has compromised my ability to attract a true partner and have the heart-fulfilling experience of being truly partnered in life.

Being a healer and providing healing has gratification, but it's an impersonal and transpersonal kind of gratification. As a conduit and a vessel, there is joy. Yet, it's not about me at a very basic human level. My best friend told me to put a note on my wall many years ago reading, "the cosmic tit is closed for business... do your own f....ing work." What a powerful prayer and affirmation to God to change the boundaries on this sacred intimate DNA template!

Becoming aware that my turning point opened a very meaningful door, but also blocked another, is perhaps part of an internal transformation. What we feel, we can heal. What we see, allows a vision of change. At this point in my life, I am almost on the other shore of a new defining moment, one of being able to be me and be loved for who I am—as a woman and as a person, by a man who stays through thick and thin. To be loved til death do us part for who I am, and not just for what I can do or give to another, is a welcome vision, an answer to a prayer.

Now I am aware of what I missed from my earlier defining moment, in addition to my gratitude for the gifts I received. And energy flows into the pathway created by awareness. I am working actively to change the DNA through my heart's consciousness, through vision and prayer. And in the process, my already wide bandwidth is growing deeper and wider.

✍

Linda Marks, MSM, is a pioneer in the field of body psychotherapy.   Founder   of   Emotional-Kinesthetic Psychotherapy, a heart-centered, psychospiritual method of body psychotherapy, she is also the co-founder of the first body psychotherapy state professional association in the country in Massachusetts in 1988. She served on the Board of the Association of Humanistic Psychology and was involved in the founding of the Somatics Community within AHP. Linda has taught in Europe and around the United States, and has presented at behavioral health, humanistic psychology and body psychotherapy conferences. She has appeared nationally on radio and television, and is the author of two books: Living With Vision: Reclaiming the Power of the Heart *(Knowledge Systems, 1988) and* Healing the War Between the Genders: The Power of the Soul-Centered Relationship *(HeartPower Press, 2004). Linda holds degrees from Yale and MIT.*

Coincidence and Transformation:
A Story of Tragedy and Triumph

Claire Beth Steinberger

"You are a fighter".
- My first psychoanalyst to me.

This clinical experience stands as the most emotionally evocative of my career, I have tears whenever I share it – filled as it is with tragedy, joy and, even, triumph. Our therapeutic encounter was a validation for my career choice, which I had been uncertain about. I believe that there was must have been some particular force that placed this patient and myself together. Our therapy made a crucial difference for him – and, in a more subtle way, for me. It was transformative.

The treatment took place while I was studying for my School Psychology Certification, a time when I was beginning analytic training and in my first analysis. My psychology internship was in a hospital for neurological diseases – a site that was hardly a first choice. Not at all. I could call it a mistake or fallback position. I remember just wanting to get it over with, especially when I initially walked into the hospital and saw long gray hallways filled with elderly people in wheelchairs – many suffering from strokes. It was jarring and, I admit, not appealing to my analytic predilections.

My twelve-month internship began in the early autumn. It had a remarkable – and still for me, almost inconceivable resolution. Somewhat magical. At my first meeting with the Department Chair, he asked me to treat a young man named Mario. I was told that he was thirty years old and had been at the hospital for about twelve years. The Chair shared very little about the patient, only his name and a skeletal picture of his life on the wards and the accident that had changed his life. I was also told he had a history of depression and periodic suicidal ideation and had been in therapy with a supervisory psychologist and several psych interns.

Mario grew up in Brooklyn. One can imagine him at age sixteen doing what many in his peer group would often do on a warm spring day – play hooky from school to go swimming at a popular nearby beach. On one particularly hot day, Mario, perhaps showing off for his friends, decided to dive into the water from the coastal rocks. On this fateful afternoon, the waves pulled back unexpectedly. Mario broke his spine and was left a quadriplegic.

I can picture Mario as a kind of rebellious street guy – a swaggering black-leather jacket teen, smoking cigarettes and carousing with his buddies. At the time of the accident, he was engaged to a dark-haired girl about his age. I see a thin-faced Sal Mineo or maybe, John Travolta.

When I first met Mario, he was lying on his stomach on a stretcher, a white sheet covering his body with only his thin face and black eyes peering up at me. He might have had a cigarette in one hand, but I am not sure. My heart stood still. I remember wanting to appear calm and receptive, while inside I was feeling shocked –horrified and overwhelmed. I do not remember the Department Chair – or anyone else – preparing me for such an emotional "confrontation". The young man on the stretcher. At that time, I was in my early to mid- thirties. We were close in age.

Two recollections stand out from the early phase of therapy. The first is the elated feeling I had when I initially saw Mario in a wheelchair. It made a big difference. As it turned out the stretcher was only employed on a temporary or emergency basis. In Mario's case, it was used to help heal the bed sores that periodically developed. It was a relief when Mario began to roll his chair into our sessions, wearing shirts and pants and smoking a cigarette, flicking the ashes into a small metal can at the end of the chair's side bar. I can still see him using his hands and wrists in a rather fast and deft way, pleased that he could get around on his own. The second memory relates to the actual treatment process, where my immediate supervisor instructed me to use only supportive therapy, for example, to "coach" Mario with daily activities.

Looking back, I believe he might have meant a form of cognitive-behavioral therapy.

Since, as I shared, I was in my own analysis at the time and was studying at an analytic institute, I decided to secretly follow my own agenda. I asked my supervisor to let me work with Mario on a twice weekly basis, choosing an insight-oriented, in-depth approach.

Although I saw Mario every week, it is almost impossible to remember the "facts" of his personal history or even much of the actual content of our sessions. He came from a small family (I never met any family members) and spoke about his fiancée -- a relationship that ended a few months after his hospitalization. I have a vague recollection of addressing his self- critical thoughts – maybe referring to a rather harsh "superego". While I do not know if this punitive voice preceded his accident, I do recollect interpreting in that sphere. As I think about it now, we might have been working on the self-flagellating thoughts that could be contributing to his depression or feelings of worthlessness. I can imagine myself challenging his attacks on his imperfect and damaged body-self, the self-criticisms that could prohibit a broader appreciation of who he was – and could be. He did not express suicidal thoughts during our time together.

What I do seem to recollect is that our therapeutic relationship took on a life of its own, something to do with the affective (intersubjective) quality of our work together. I can recall Mario beginning to wear bright flowered shirts and sometimes wheeling into the sessions with his head tilted to one side, carrying a wise-guy seductive kind of smile. There was at least one occasion where he teasingly challenged me, rolling the wheelchair around the desk, as if trying to pin me in. I remember trying to hold a somewhat serious or professional countenance. I was not sure what to do. Could I have smiled in an embarrassed or self-conscious way or maybe blushed? I do know that I did not want to hurt him, cutting off his masculine (if somewhat inappropriate) behaviors. These sexual and emotionally-charged images remain fresh, along with my reckoning of how to move sensitively through this tangle of erotic advances that felt so out of place, and so relevant.

At some point during the early months of the internship, I had this unexpected thought. I told myself that I would get Mario out of the hospital before my internship ended, that is, by the end of the following summer. I was not ambivalent. To this day, I have no inkling of how this far-fetched idea developed. I can simply say that just a few years after the internship terminated, I shared this private "contract" with Doctor Norman Ackerman, a gifted training psychiatrist at Bronx Psychiatric Family Study Section. He found that this sort of unwavering determination – an unconsciously informed "knowing" -- had unusual power or predictive meaning. I have never had such a purposive feeling about anything else in my life. It was a different kind of knowing. Today, I think that my vision – a wish for Mario to "make it" – came from a side of myself (an internal voice) that still believes that people can overcome the near-impossible – move mountains – where internal conflict or unconscious ambivalence does not stand in the way. Perhaps I experienced Mario's masculine, somewhat omnipotent quality as expressing a significant and authentic part of his identity.   A fighter – a man seeking to live, to go out into the world.

Here was a guy who wanted to fly -- to touch, to contact, to have sex -- and I (unconsciously) connected and identified…and needed to make it happen.

As the treatment progressed, I continued what I thought was a "classical" or more traditional approach, investigating Mario's history and the fantasies he had of himself, the accident, the loss of his girlfriend, and so forth. Perhaps I worked with some dreams, as well. I believe I also modeled myself on my own analyst and his quiet reflective kind of listening. I cannot recall how I addressed our relationship (or even if I did), but I do know that I never upset some aspect of the transference or relational experience that was bringing him back to life.   There was much that was left unsaid. This might have been intuitive or from a lack of experience on my part. As I look back, I believe that the silent world – the relational unconscious – was doing much of the work.

During one spring afternoon therapy session, Mario reported unexpected news. He was attending a daily recreational rehab program and one of the female therapists had fallen in love with him. The couple was planning to take an apartment outside the hospital grounds. I was taken aback. I am embarrassed to admit that at first glance I did not really believe him – or was concerned that he was imagining or embellishing some wish-fulfilling interchange.

Mario had not said much about this specific woman or, if he had, I missed the import of their relationship. (I now ask, was he protecting his self-esteem by not sharing more with me until he was more certain? Was he working through an unconscious struggle between this "new" woman and his dark-haired fiancé and/or therapist?) We planned a couple's session for the end of the week. I was unsure what would emerge. Finally, they were there before me, Mario in his wheelchair and the young woman sitting on his right side. They were calm and smiling. She was an attractive blond-haired American woman who had graduated from a prestigious college a few years earlier. While I privately questioned the meaning of her decision and the unusual path she was choosing, I knew she meant business. I did not want to delve too deeply into her personal history, most likely afraid of upsetting the applecart.

A few weeks after this session, they left the hospital together. It was approximately two weeks before my internship terminated.

Several months later, a close friend who was shopping in a popular clothing store in the city decided to stop for coffee in a nearby diner. She happened to overhear a woman in the next booth discussing a man named Mario. Unable to resist, my friend turned to ask if this could be the very same Mario who had left the hospital. The woman answered excitedly, "Yes, tell Claire we are both fine and doing well".

Tears come to my eyes as I write these words...so many years later.

In sharing these recollections, I have let my feelings lead the way.

I will add little of my own developmental history, only that I grew up in Brooklyn, a dark-haired, dark eyed girl who was somewhat social and gregarious as well as self-reflective and introspective. As a child, I struggled with separation issues, reflecting a close, if not overly-enmeshed mother-daughter relationship with heightened social and 'perfectionistic' delineations. I was also "father's little girl' and had a seductive narcissistic father that I adored. Clearly, a range of developmental strivings and identifications were triggered by the work with this patient.

It is most probable, as well, that my relatively young and inexperienced analytic self was "right" for this job, freeing me for this dynamic and unchartered "force field".

Finally, I continue to feel that some mysterious hand was at work, placing this patient and myself in each other's path. The "horror" that I felt when first seeing Mario came from a pivotal place in my own psyche.

My own background gave rise to childhood struggles related to separation and rigid expectations regarding physical attraction and "perfection" and social approval. They formed the essence of storylines – the unspoken rules and judgments that could guide my dreams and self –delineations.

The relationship with my mother was "overly enmeshed", and I was "daddy's little girl" too. In effect, my internal world was filled with heightened anxiety regarding my physical appearance and competitive competency. I can remember trying to soothe my own precarious self-assurance and esteem by telling myself, "I will be okay no matter what I wear", a few days prior to my eleven- year- old birthday party. When my mother died suddenly of advanced colon cancer when I was sixteen years old (the same age of Mario's accident), I was at the height of an adolescent struggle, marked by over-zealous dating and beauty competitions.

My mother's death had a crippling effect on my development. (When I was twenty-two I went on a trip abroad with friends, and I can remember borrowing a shawl from a handicapped young woman and my dread at actually wearing it – an object that had 'absorbed' the deformity; putting it on made me feel handicapped too.

My clinical work with this quadriplegic man, so close to my own age, challenged my vulnerable feelings about physical attractiveness, social approval and competitive possibility. Like Mario, I tended to criticize and devalue myself. Mario's treatment required me to dig into a number of dreaded places. I would need to open a path for my own growth – an analytic re-birth and discovery.

Mario's therapy was a lightning rod that triggered a journey into my own psychic arrests and entrapment. The therapeutic relationship could be understood as a working-through of the "trauma" of being with Mario – and, of being with myself – meeting some split-off frightened and insecure voices inside my own psyche. Delving into myself meant confronting the critical and perfectionistic (mother-daughter) constellations – battles between the inner and outer, perfect and imperfect and, ultimately, the assertive and risk-taking and the compliant (enmeshed) self-representations.

I believe that Mario's deep black eyes, with their imploring and seductive qualities kindled my own identifications. I wonder, was it my father's eyes or even my own that were familiar to me, now reflected in this dyadic "force field"? I remember the look in Mario's eyes as he first searched my face, "hooking" on to some part of me that would respond with affirmation and approval. Why did I not "fold" or go into hiding as I did with the lady with the shawl (cited earlier). Why did he strike the chord that made me bold? Was my response a healthy form of grandiosity – some ambitious or independent identification?

I was there and would not let him down. I can imagine that we were in some 'mutual field' – teens together, sharing some social and sexual identifications, playing hooky (where the parents, teachers and administrators would not tread). Although I was, in most ways, my mother's narcissistic extension (the beautiful and popular daughter), could I also be the seductive and charismatic daughter, responding to her father and an admiring aspect of her mother – a more individuated oedipal organization? Did my healthier sexual self-resonate with Mario's pre-traumatized self? Did I affirm his assertiveness and masculinity?

As a child and later, as a teenager and young adult, I struggled to achieve a solid sense of autonomy, fighting the pull of maternal enmeshment. Identifying with Mario, I shared the feeling of wanting to go out – to go forward…and the horror of being frozen and stuck.

The need to continue to move on -- to foster my own separate choices (boundaries) -- to feel safe in my own (psychic) skin were recurrent themes in my personal analysis. In an uncanny way, Mario's healthy aggressive (active) self-imago was also "trapped", subjected to a damaged body and changed self-representations, where shame and rage would dominate the loss of former masculine and ejaculatory functions. Although I experienced a different form of incapacitation, Mario's struggle resonated with my own dread of dependency, immobility and psychic "arrest". I shared the fear of social isolation, a wallflower who could lose out – unable to blossom and grow.

I was in touch with a desire to fight for my own survival, to break free from my mother and live my life. I remember my analyst at that time stating, "Even a fly fights for its life". Although he was speaking to my personal struggles, the associations came through in my therapeutic work with Mario. Along this line, I believe that my private contract and unwavering conviction, "He will leave this hospital before I do", suggests that Mario (and I) will—and must – get out! My quest to step out into the world was there since childhood, an unresolved battle that remained well after my mother's untimely death. I was ready for Mario.

Both Mario and I knew the meaning of arrested development. Mario's arrest was particularly rooted to physical trauma, an external assault that appeared to fall upon "good enough" self and object internalizations. My own arrest, on the other hand, was haunted by pathological and inhibiting internalizations. In Loewald's (1977) terms, this treatment opened the way for each of us to become "new objects" for identification, the opportunity for psychic development.

I continue to hold Mario in a heroic place, an admired model (internalization) of what can be – there for the fighting versions of myself. The stuff of dreams...

Book quoted: LOEWALD, H. (1977). Primary process, secondary process and language. In Papers on psychoanalysis (pp.178-206). New Haven, CT: Yale University Press, 1980. (1960). The therapeutic relationship. In Papers on psychoanalysis.

I would like to dedicate this paper to my sister Ruth Hildy, a woman who actualizes "impossible" dreams, making this world a kinder and better place – and beating the odds.

I also want to thank Dr. Ahron Friedberg and the American Society of Psychoanalytic Physicians for their generous comments regarding a draft presentation of this paper, October 4, 2012.

Claire Beth Steinberger has a Doctoral Degree from Columbia University Teachers College. She is Psychologist (NJS), Supervisory School Psychologist (NYS), Psychoanalyst, Supervisory Member American Association Marriage and Family Therapy, Mediator and Parent Coordinator. She is faculty at National Psychological Association of Psychoanalysis, Training Institute Mental Health, Program in Family Law and Family Forensics. Specializations: Psychoanalysis and Family Systems, Child and Adolescent Development, and Family-School Collaboration. Adjunct Faculty, Long Island University, New York University and Brooklyn College. She was Clinical Supervisor, Family Counseling Program, NYC Board of Education, Senior Psychologist, John F. Kennedy Medical Center (NJ), Supervisor, Object Relations Institute. Interdisciplinary clinical research includes Teenage Depression: A Cultural-Interpersonal-Intrapsychic Perspective *(1989);* Therapeutic Jurisprudence *(2003);* Cyberspace *(2009). Recent presentations,* A Journey Through Systems *(Spring 2012), IFPE, Mt. Sinai Psychotherapy Faculty Group. (Text in process: Psychoanalytic- Systems Interface). She has a private practice, New York and New Jersey.*

From Sponge to Firm Container:
A Therapist Grows in New York

Cheryl Dolinger Brown

I grew up in the Midwest in a loving, middle-class Jewish family full of teachers and social workers. From the time I was little I knew I was meant to do something important in my life, to take care of people and help make a better world. After my father died suddenly when I was ten I took on the job of caring for those close to me, especially when they were depressed and vulnerable. As an adult I am able to see the magical thinking I developed back then: I believed that I could alleviate people's hurt and pain by absorbing some of it myself and then nurturing them. As I received appreciation for my care of others, I became convinced that it was acceptable and admirable to take care of other people's needs even if it was at my own expense. If others needed me I felt that I was safe, necessary, and loved, and would not be abandoned. These childhood adaptations groomed me for the work that has become my passion. They also set me up to hold unrealistic standards for myself that were not helpful in my work with trauma.

I graduated with my Masters in Social Work in 1975. Growing up I knew very little about psychotherapy, but in New York City a large number of my classmates planned to continue their postgraduate studies in psychoanalytic institutes and develop private practices. Psychoanalysis was highly respected in the field. Most medical insurances reimbursed clients for weekly sessions, and managed care had not yet begun to wrest control over the treatment that could be provided.

I was originally introduced to psychoanalysis through the therapist I was assigned to at a clinic and I followed in her footsteps at the institute where she was involved. I studied and practiced psychoanalysis for many years, but was never entirely comfortable within that framework. The method felt too distant and intellectual for my personality and over time I became more eclectic in my beliefs and skills. I continued my studies for twelve years because I was persistent and needed to feel a sense of completion. What a relief it was in 1995 to be exposed to Imago Relationship Therapy and to be trained in a method where I could work and relate in a more down to earth manner, to be more directive in my coaching of couples. It was also important for me to find a professional community where I felt accepted and safe. So much of the work in the office is solitary; being in a community through training, workshops, chapter meetings, peer groups and annual conferences provided me with a sense of community. I found a group where I felt safe and connected yet encouraged to live at my growth edge. I have practiced Imago for seventeen years as an advanced clinician and consultant (supervisor).

Years later, in 2003, I found Somatic Experiencing transformative during a personal crisis. The SE therapist helped me tolerate the fear I was experiencing and at the same time find a more complete way to resolve past traumas that I had worked on in psychoanalysis and in additional psychodynamic therapy. This body-based therapy helped me connect what I already knew intellectually with my bodily sensations and I learned to calm my nervous system. I subsequently trained as a certified Somatic Experiencing Practitioner.

During thirty-two years of private therapy practice, I have had four traumatized clients who were horrifically abused for extended periods of time during childhood; they strongly challenged my predisposition to be a sponge for absorbing pain. This is the story of my personal and professional transformation, my journey to become a better therapist and more balanced human being. My greatest challenge was learning to set firm boundaries while retaining my empathy and to find hope in the midst of trauma and pain.

It was 1980 and I was twenty-eight years old when Bella walked into the closet- sized office I was renting by the hour. I was no longer the naive adult I had been when I left Minneapolis and arrived in New York City for graduate school. But two years of graduate school and five years working in a foster care agency left me woefully unprepared to be a witness to her horrifying story, to tolerate the intensity of her pain and the rage in our relationship, or to have the skills to deal with the trauma.

Twenty-one year old Bella was referred to me for low cost psychoanalytic psychotherapy. With high levels of anxiety and anger and great difficulty getting along with others, she had begun her first job after graduating from college. Her scared, angry eyes and persistent scowl took away from her attractiveness and beautiful red hair. She had little money and few social supports. She reported feeling in continual psychic pain, as if she was walking around the world with no skin to protect her.

We worked together twice a week for ten years and what emerged was a childhood history of outrageous cruelty, of extreme physical, emotional and sexual abuse by her father, a member of the clergy. The memories and stories came up gradually through flashbacks, dreams and in her creative work. I helped her through three psychiatric hospitalizations for serious self-mutilation (cutting). The two to three week-long hospitalizations gave her a relatively safe place to stabilize. They also gave me a brief time to ground myself and take a break from the constant worry but the stays were never long enough for her to get much treatment. The medications did not work and the staff did not help us develop good discharge plans. Unfortunately, there were few behavioral treatment programs for Post-Traumatic Stress Disorder in our country at that time.

I was totally in the dark about how to help with the self-mutilation. No supervisor or teacher I consulted knew how to deal with it; There was no Google or Amazon in those days to find resources and there were no "made for TV" movies that brought self-abuse out of the closet. Helping her make the connection between her present behavior and how she was harmed as a child did not lessen the pain or compulsion. Bella was open to journaling and drawing when upset but self-injury was the only way she could dissociate from the emotional pain and obtain relief. I tried to think of other ways for her to soothe herself, but lacked the knowledge and skills to help her in her most severe states.

One day she brought a package of razors to session. She planned to cut herself with them but instead threw them down on the table between us. I took them, telling her I would keep them to help her stay safe. For a while she carried a pocketknife to protect herself from danger; she gave it to me when she had a strong impulse to cut herself. We both knew that taking these instruments from her was only a symbol— she could get more any time—but by handing them over she felt like someone cared. I felt like I was literally and figuratively putting a bandage on a gaping wound and felt helpless to do more, but over the years she alluded to the fact that I helped keep her alive.

Being in the same room with Bella was difficult for the first six or seven years. She often saw me as the terrifying and brutal father or her disengaged mother who could not protect her. At different times in the course of treatment, I would play different roles in the transference which was confusing and upsetting to me. I was the recipient of the hatred and rage that she had experienced growing up. I often disappointed her and she was frequently angry with me. Anger was never expressed directly in my family and was frightening to me. I would often get butterflies in my stomach when I anticipated her anger. I imagined a parallel process here where she gave me a taste of the feelings she experienced as a child at the hand of her father.

When she dissociated in session I saw her disappear and could no longer feel her presence in the room with me. I felt frightened since attuning to her feelings was a way for me to sense what was happening and without it I felt lost. When she disappeared behind her eyes I didn't knowing how to get her back into the present. I watched her terror when she slipped into the abyss and I felt like I was trying to hold on to her as she was drowning, crying out to me for help. I experienced her infantile urge to destroy my power in the countertransference: I felt powerless, hopeless and incompetent when she reproached me for not helping her feel better. The profession lacked the knowledge of trauma and skills that we now have which would have helped her and me.

Sometimes I actually felt some relief and, of course, guilt, when she did cut herself; with it she experienced a release from the building, unrelenting torment. Sometimes therapy helped her soothe herself but the pain reliably diminished for a while after the "blood-letting." She was able to clean and bandage her wounds if they were minor. Even though I couldn't help her stop, it was important that she didn't have to hide the shameful behavior from me as she did from everyone else. Once she called me after cutting herself and it sounded severe to me. She followed my direction and went to the emergency room. It wasn't until 1994 when I read Dusty Miller's book *Women Who Hurt Themselves: A Book Of Hope And Understanding*, that I learned that "self-injury activates endorphins that actually calm the psychic pain of old wounds."

Bella would 'know" me, Cheryl, but sometimes couldn't remember me or hold on to me when not in session. At the beginning of sessions for couple years, I would try to remind her of a connection we had, something we had discussed or shared. It was frustrating for me to feel that we had developed an understanding or connection by the end of the session just to see it disappear by the next.

I became pregnant just a few months after I started my work with Bella and our work continued until my daughter was ten years old. Bella had difficulty holding onto me during the year that my daughter began part-time day care. It was my daughter's first big separation from me and she was helped by her transitional objects: a bottle and a doll. So physical touchstones, transitional objects, were on my mind. I gave Bella a small rock from my office and she took a Polaroid picture of me to help her remember our connection. She wrote a poem that helped her to connect to me. It was not about the calm blue lakes and green trees that I feel connected to, but vibrant sunsets of orange, pink and fiery red that represented the passion and vibrancy she saw in me. In this she found a creative and more permanent way to internalize me.

Bella felt alone and, in reality, was on her own. Her reality was such a clear parallel to my experience. I felt alone with her despite the fact that I was taking classes in analytic training, working in my own analysis, and participating in individual and group supervision and peer groups. The psychoanalytic approach was not helpful enough and the field of trauma was only in its infancy. I referred Bella to psychiatrist after psychiatrist. They didn't last very long as each found her too difficult to work with. Unfortunately, no psychotropic medication was helpful.

One helpful art therapist Bella met during her last hospitalization worked with her for two years as an outpatient adjunct to our therapy. It was a good experience for Bella since she used her art as a way to express her feelings and understand herself. During that time I no longer felt alone. I conferred with someone who knew what it felt like to be in the room with her, someone who could give me a brief "oasis" from being the only one supporting Bella.

It was painful for me to bear witness to the unspeakable horror, sadism, betrayal and aloneness she had been exposed to as a child. She felt unreachable and untouchable, and I knew that I was often the only person she had to hold onto. I felt my inability to help her as a personal failing. Sometimes I felt trapped and resentful since I could not envision a positive future for her and imagined us locked in our difficult therapeutic relationship forever. A hero in Alistair MacLean's The Dark Crusader (1961:129) describes the frustration I felt: "the urgency so desperate, the progress so infuriatingly slow."

When Bella started remembering and talking about specific memories of abuse she would shake, and my words could not soothe her. For a few months, I sat next to her on the couch, sometimes touching her hand or shoulder for support. Although it was not an accepted practice in my psychoanalytic training, I saw that it helped her. I wondered if the strict doctrines of psychoanalysis were inappropriate for severe trauma work. Bella needed real human contact. It made it safer for her to keep exploring the frightening memories and feelings that arose. Throughout her childhood Bella learned to be hyper-vigilant. Her father was violent and unpredictable and she watched out for the dangerous attacks. Many of them happened in the middle of the night when she was startled out of her sleep. She grew up with a nervous system that was never at rest, and remembering those childhood events in session triggered her into the old alert state of panic. Although I did not then know how to help her ground and center herself, I realize that by sitting next to her she "entrained" to my more organized (although not always calmer) nervous system.

The hardest times for me were when my daughter was three or four; that was the age that Bella's father had begun his abuse. As some of her memories got clearer and clearer I would look at my precious, well-loved child and imagine how horrible it must have been for Bella. I didn't want her abuse and tragedies to intrude on my life, but it was impossible not to make some connections between my child and my client who was so hurt at the same age. I was happy and busy being a mother, wife and psychotherapist and I was not entirely overcome by her pain. Although my supervisors and colleagues told me to distance myself from the pain, I truly didn't know how to do that. My adaptation in life was to feel another's pain and needs and I couldn't figure out how to create a boundary as others advised me.

Without experience I couldn't see the path ahead of us or believe that she could get better. In 1991 I read an article in the November/December issue of *Family Therapy Networker* by Jeffery Jay that resonated with me and that I held onto like a talisman. He explained that no one wants to hear the traumatized client's "terrible knowledge" because it destroys our essential beliefs about human beings and life. He described how the client feels terrified, confused, isolated and alienated by memories of abuse that no one else knows about or believes:

...what if the hope that is so central to therapy denies the client's fundamental experience of reality, contradicts memories so horrifying that they annihilate any belief in the trustworthiness of the world? ... hope is the sovereign prescription for the very condition that makes hope impossible... we help them speak out with courage and honesty about their knowledge of life's darkness. Trauma survivors have experienced what none choose, and many refuse to see. ... If we listen without fear... perhaps together we can discover the possibility for honest hope, uncompromised with denial and falseness." (p. 39)

Twenty years later I can still quote these passages verbatim. That reveals to me how alone I felt at the time and how much I needed to know that being present and witnessing her pain could make a difference.

Bella had courage and persistence. Over the years we both learned how to help her articulate the unspeakable pain. Movement, collage and poetry were more useful to her than talking and were the most grounding way for her to express herself. She brought in her work to many sessions for us to discuss. I've kept a collage she gave me of her negative introjects with a small image of hope at the bottom. Threatening figures loom over a small child; nearby a small flower is beginning to blossom and a hand, mine, is reaching for her. I cared deeply about her and kept working with her. For ten years she kept coming to therapy and she slowly progressed.

I acknowledged when I misunderstood or hurt her and worked to make repairs. We developed a shared history together and she learned how to be in a relationship through our connection. I appreciated her artistry and sometimes we had sessions with more lightness and humor. Her life started getting better, although it was difficult for her to share the positive changes with me for a long time. She stayed away from her parents who made her feel crazy and developed a relationship with, and ultimately married, a man who cared for her and knew her history.

What was therapeutically healing was my constancy in trying to understand her and the impact of the abuse. Despite my periodic wish to run away, my inherent persistence prevailed. After she moved out of town she continued to stay in touch with me periodically, updating me on her marriage, progressing artwork, and after her father's death, a reconnection with her mother. I often think of her. She found a permanent place in my heart.

It is impossible for me to view my internal changes in dealing with trauma without putting it into a social context. In the mid-seventies when I finished graduate school, feminist organizations hosted speak-outs of women's lives that openly revealed how prevalent the "secret" acts of rape, domestic violence and incest were against children and women of all socioeconomic, racial and religious groups. It seemed to me that Freud was originally correct in assuming that many of the hysterical symptoms he was seeing were due to incest and rape. I also understand why he recanted his theory due to public and professional pressure. Although my intensive training in psychoanalysis gave me a firm foundation in understanding unconscious processes, dream analysis, transference and counter-transference, the style of relating felt too emotionally distant and did not suit my personality or my burgeoning beliefs about healing.

The 1980's and 1990's was a time of panic over the False Memory Syndrome. Many abuse cases came to light in the public, descriptions of "upstanding citizens" involving children in sexual and physical abuse, brainwashing, pornography, prostitution, and ritual abuse. The numbers and types of abuse cases reported were seen by many in the public as being the products of suggestive techniques used by therapists. The panic affected lawyers, therapists, social workers and the courts and made the study and treatment of psychological trauma highly controversial. I understood why it was so hard for the public to believe these sensational reports; it was for me too. At times it was also confusing to know what to believe of my client's memories since they were often unclear and came out in diffuse associations. I felt like a detective, looking for patterns and consistencies and trying to understand how her present symptoms and defenses developed from the abuse.

In 1991 I joined a supervision group to examine Judith Lewis Herman's groundbreaking book, "Trauma and Recovery." We read and discussed her book chapter by chapter which finally put into context much of what seemed confusing in treatment and pointed a path toward recovery from the abuse.

The field of family systems was burgeoning but there was very little information disseminated about handling trauma. I read voraciously, finding a few books that provided knowledge and affirmation for me. The most important ones that helped me were *The Drama of the Gifted Child*, by Alice Miller (1979), *People of the Lie*, by M. Scott Peck (1982), *The Courage to Heal*, by Ellen Bass and Laura Davis (1988) and *Soul Murder*, by Leonard Shengold (1991). These books were important to me because I had I felt great repulsion and even hatred of the perpetrator of the violence directed at my client. Although I wished I had never been exposed to it, I needed to understand the sadism. At first my curiosity and understanding was intellectual. It took me many years to understand that I was looking at my shadow, my denied self. I didn't want to believe that hatred, anger, meanness and a desire to hurt existed in me. Being mean was the strongest taboo of my childhood, and yet, the feelings of wanting to hurt Bella's father were stimulated in me. I didn't want to hurt my client, but when she raged at me for long periods of time I did wish she would leave me. Another article which resonated with me and that I reread several times was D. W. Winnicott's "Hate in the Countertransference." Coming to terms with my strong negative feelings, accepting them with compassion for myself, has been an important and continuing process in my growth both personally and professionally.

Times have changed again. Many prominent people such as religious figures, politicians and athletes have been exposed and the details of their sexual, emotional and/or physical abuse of those with lesser power have been in the media. Although the victims are still often blamed and ridiculed, many more people are aware of the incomprehensible acts and the cover-ups and many former victims have come forward. There is stronger public belief that such acts exist and that they have tremendous ongoing impact on the victims. From that has come some legal reform.

During the last twenty years the field of trauma has advanced. While working with two more severely traumatized clients, many of my fundamental assumptions about healing changed and they have reshaped my interventions. "Working through" the abuse by talking about it is inadequate. Through the years I've seen that in therapy, one size does not fit all, and focusing on the body must be a part of the work. Through my own practice of Somatic Experiencing, yoga, meditation and the tapping EFT method, I work with the body as well as the mind and emotions of my clients. By using Somatic Experiencing I have learned how to ground and soothe myself, to contain my reactivity and stay within the bounds of my resilience, even when faced with a person in great pain in front of me. What I have learned is not only intellectual, but is embodied in my presence. Because of that I am able to listen to my client's "terrible knowledge" in a way that is solid. I can truly be present without losing my center. A traumatized client needs to have a witness and has to believe that I can listen to her story without recoiling, minimizing or falling apart. This gives her permission and invites her to be real and present despite overwhelming fear and shame.

Yoga has also helped me bring body awareness into therapy sessions. Uncomfortable yoga poses cause a loss of connection to what is available in the moment and there is an urge to move out of them. Learning to breathe through the sensation helps one stay grounded in the present. If a pose is too hard, a person can learn to stop fighting and back off. I use this image with clients. There is a clear parallel with staying with intense emotions and painful sensations. In sessions I use certain poses when a client feels weak, scared or dissociated. We stand together in the middle of the room in Mountain Pose or Warrior Two until she feels her energy return and feels grounded enough to find her source of strength. My personal meditation practice is also useful in teaching breathing techniques and finding ways to let go of critical and negative thoughts. I have continually worked on shoring up my boundaries. And in a parallel process, that is exactly what my clients also have to learn. Who better to teach than one who has struggled with similar issues and learned to overcome them?

In the last two years I have been working with a client in her twenties whose work highlights changes in the way I now practice therapy and the way I care for myself. From the time she was a preschooler through mid-adolescence Colleen was sexually abused by her father and sadistically abused by her stepmother. Our work has a life-and-death feel to it: she is physically ill from childhood mistreatment and emotionally vulnerable after years of brainwashing. After a recent rape by a person that she trusted that was similar to past experiences and reawakened her original trauma, she has been self-abusive. She is a resilient and beautiful soul who is persevering and working very hard to strengthen herself and heal through therapy. Although it is an emotionally difficult case for me, I don't feel continually overwhelmed as I did with Bella.

It is easier to teach techniques to her when I myself have found help with them. I've taught Colleen how to use her physical sensations as important signals to heed and to use body-focused techniques to release the trauma that is trapped in her nervous system. When she is triggered I slow her down knowing that she is able to tolerate only a limited amount of the difficult feelings before catapulting into panic or dissociation. I sit with her and she feels my presence as she is in terror. She is able to tolerate the spikes of feeling, the sensations and emotions, a little longer each time. In this way we are re-teaching her nervous system to regulate itself, to go from fight/flight response into a state of greater calm. Slowing down her story to pay attention to her body also creates a space for me to ground and regulate myself, especially after hearing a gruesome story or witnessing her pain.

Dissociation happens very quickly. I used to be very frightened when the light went out of Bella's eyes. She seemed so out of my reach and I wanted to get her out of the state immediately, but didn't know how to help. I am not afraid of Colleen's dissociation, but respect it as a necessary defense and phase. I know that the emotions and sensations are too intense in the moment and that I can help her tolerate what has come up. Now that I have techniques to help Colleen be more present, I am confident that with time she will return to a regulated state. Because she is attuning to my energy, my staying calm helps her find a calmer state also.

Bearing witness to horror can lead to "secondary traumatization" or "compassion fatigue." For a long time in my career I did not realize how important self-care was as an antidote to burn-out. My identity was wrapped up in being "small but strong", someone who could handle what might be too difficult for others. I became known as a therapist who could take on cases others didn't want. I was used to pushing myself to take on harder and harder challenges, an adaptation that caused me to ignore my own needs. I was being pulled into what, in Somatic Experiencing, is called a familiar "trauma vortex." At one point early in my career when I was working with Bella I considered leaving the field. I was worried that I was too weak to listen to the pain and trauma. I wondered if I was inadequate, if there was something missing in me that made me unable to "fix" a hurting person. I had even more questions about why I could not let go of their pain as other therapists seemed to do. I am very glad now that I gave it another chance and learned to take better care of my physical and emotional needs.

I learned how to balance my life as a full-time therapist. I continue to thrive on the intensity of psychotherapy but know that I required a balance of quiet, contemplative time. I must sit on the grass under a tree and daydream, read, meditate and do creative activities such as beading jewelry. I need physical exercise to feel good and I find it in regular yoga classes in the middle of my work day. I need a great deal of social connection and meet frequently with friends and colleagues. Throughout my career I have continuously been in individual and group supervision, peer groups, trainings and workshops, and professional associations. I also give myself variety and adventure, whether it is a trip abroad or walking in a new neighborhood in the city. Every Monday I buy myself beautiful roses for the office. These things nourish me and show me the beauty in life. I tell Colleen about some of these activities as we explore hers. I model how to live a more satisfying life, something she never felt she deserved.

I handle my private practice differently now knowing that I can't and shouldn't do it alone. Working in private practice does not give the structure that a clinic or hospital does. I am continually working with Colleen to find resources to help her. I encourage her to put together a support team for medical, legal, home health aid and community/friendship relationships. Because she does not feel deserving and feels she has to pay penance for being a bad person, she has difficulty asking for and then using help. Although this is slow work, having her find help in others rather than trying to fill all roles is an important part of her therapy and my self-care.

Another way I protect myself from being overwhelmed with the pain is by choosing to have only one or two clients at a time in my practice who are experiencing the life-and-death dramas that come with recovering from long- term childhood trauma. When I was triggered by a recent rape Colleen experienced, I stopped taking new clients for a couple of months. I cut down on the normally small amounts of news that I listen to so I could protect myself until I felt less vulnerable. I needed to experience less stress, so I took on less rather than more. This is different from my past behavior.

Because I am able to nurture and nourish myself, my creativity is more accessible in sessions with Colleen. Creativity expresses a strong life force, a contradiction to the "soul murder" that takes place in ongoing child abuse. Creativity is so essential in seeing life in a new way, in allowing for full expression and passion in life, and in teaching her how to be firmly planted in the present. It also brings liveliness into sessions, something we both need to access. During sessions we draw images with magic markers and write down significant ideas for her to take home. We've come up with songs or movies that perfectly expressed the theme of the day or ones that make her feel stronger. Colleen saves all of our notes and pictures in a package and carries them around with her to read when she gets confused or needs emotional sustenance.

Humor, especially dark humor, helps us both out. The humor dispels fear and shame and if there is anything to laugh at, we find it. There are sessions when we laugh until we cry, stimulating our endorphins and creating a bond between us; sometimes, "girls just want to have fun."

Being direct, not in a hurtful way but with clarity and honesty, makes it easier for me to be real and solid and prevents me from sinking into my client's feelings. At times she sees my genuine feelings: sadness, indignation on her behalf, fury at the predator who assaulted her. Since she did not have appropriate emotions and responses mirrored for her while she was growing up, it is essential that she sees mine. It allows her to access her feelings, even when she is afraid or judgmental of them. She has responded: "if you feel this way, maybe I am not such a horrible person for having these feelings." If she asks about a look on my face, the truthfulness of my response creates a sense of safety, even if it includes information that is hard for her to hear.

What is it that has helped me in my transformation that can be passed on to other therapists? If I accept that people aren't fixable and know my own limits, then my job is to orient them to and prompt their own healing capabilities. I can be a witness to the horrors of their past when I keep myself grounded. I have learned that sometimes people need therapy as a support network to hold on to life until the context of their life changes and improves. A month ago I heard from Bella. She knew she could not and should not have children, but sent a picture of herself and her husband looking so happy with her two nieces. She continues to paint, sculpt and do photography, promotes her artwork on- line, and reports that she has developed a better relationship with her mother. She says that our work feels like another lifetime ago. It does to me, too.

Even when it feels like an uphill battle I can now hold onto my hope for my clients and our work together. It is so important for them to feel this from me. Through the years I have experienced the resilience and motivation in many of my clients. I have respect for them when they don't give up. Even in a life of pain, letting go of the tight hold of the past, not indulging in the anxiety of the future, and being in the moment can bring moments of quiet. As Colleen looks at herself and her past through my eyes, not those of her internalized negative parents, she is able to claim her competence. She has moments of "grace" when she feels calm, gratitude and a new sense of belonging. Deep in her heart she knows how dangerous and hurtful people can be and she is opening to kindness and expansiveness and engaging in vital relationships. She is in transition, experiencing the trauma from the past while dreaming of her better future.

It has taken an entire adulthood to strengthen my boundaries so that I can hold onto myself in the face of the pain of those I care about. It has certainly taken patience and self-compassion to work on the vulnerable and unpleasant parts of myself. I have learned how to dip into another's world of pain and then pull away from it--a hard trick to learn. It has certainly been worth the journey for me to be empathic and connected while staying separate, whole and grounded. And I feel blessed to have accompanied my courageous clients on their journeys to a safer, fuller life.

Cheryl Dolinger Brown, LCSW, has been practicing as a psychotherapist in New York City for over thirty years with individuals, couples and groups in addition to presenting workshops and supervising therapists. She was Director of Wellness Services in a national Employee Assistance Program, developing and presenting over 45 corporate wellness seminars. She has written articles for the magazine Social Work Today *and was an advisor on their editorial board. She believes in life-long learning and has been certified as a Psychoanalyst, Imago Relationship Therapist (advanced clinician and consultant), and a Somatic Experience Practitioner. Since a balanced life is so important to her, she practices yoga and meditation, cooks and bakes, creates jewelry in a weekly beading group and loves playing with friends and family.*

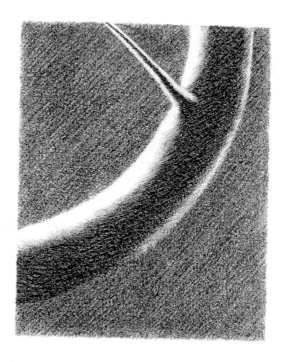

Lucid Therapy

Lou Hagood

For years I have practiced dream incubation and lucid dreaming on my own, keeping it separate from my psychotherapy practice. Clients bring in dreams, which we use in the therapy work in traditional ways. I felt it was sufficient that I suggested dreams as material for our work without stretching the point to include the more esoteric dream practices, and besides, it took many years of my own therapy before I developed those esoteric practices myself. A couple of years ago, a client I will call Dan dreamed that his dying mother took his hand. The mother died right after that, and at the next session I said it was good that he had the dream before she died.

Over the next few months, Dan had a couple of dreams of his mother, confused, at the front door of his childhood home, trying to get in. Then he said that he never told his mother that her approval didn't matter anymore, just the love they had. From my experiences with the beyond in dream-incubation questions and lucidity, it seemed to me that his departed mother was trying to make contact with him. In my lucid dreams of

departed family, I had found the encounters
therapeutic and helpful in moving on with my life. In
one dream my deceased aunt had given me advice on a
therapy client that aided me in our work. I sensed that
Dan's mother was knocking at his door in dreams for
similar assistance. I hesitated for a moment, then said,
"Tell her in your dreams."

I was reluctant to push him, but it was the only
way that he could communicate to her how he felt, and
get her assistance in moving on with his life. Dan and I
came from church-going families, but had forsaken the
church as adults, so our access to the beyond was not
in church but in dreams. From the start of our work
together, Dan had started most sessions with a dream,
which we referred to throughout the hour, so I had
faith in his facility with the dream world.

The next session Dan told me that he was
becoming conscious in his dreams, especially when
awakening in the morning, which I recognized as the
liminal space where communication with the beyond
occurs. It was reassuring that my encouragement to
communicate with his mother in dreams was not "wild
therapy", but a suggestion that was resulting in an
evolution of dream consciousness that could facilitate
contact with the beyond.

I felt that he was ready for the next step in
responding to his mother and was excited about the
development. I suggested that he could tell his mother
how he felt in those conscious moments, using his
terminology of "the twilight zone" instead of my own.

"You mean I could have an exit interview with my mother?" There followed a dream in which his mother called on the phone and he talked to her briefly.

Dan was in an acupuncture session shortly thereafter, when in a trance state he felt his mother's hand on his right leg. "I went in and out of the trance with her hand pressure," he said. I suggested that the twilight zone when he is conscious in his dreams when awakening in the morning is a similar trance state where he can be in touch with his mother, using his terminology, once again, following his and his mother's lead, rather than directing the show myself.

My suggestion that Dan tell his departed mother how he feels about her in his dreams was a departure from traditional dream work in therapy. After the passing of a loved one, their appearance in dreams triggers conscious and unconscious memories and feelings that aid in the grieving process. This makes the therapy focused on the past.

Lucidity, both waking and sleeping, implies being in the present, not in a replay of the past or hopes for the future. Regardless of whether present reality is external or an internal image, lucidity requires an encounter in the present moment. Visitations from the dead can be a return from the beyond or be unconscious images, but lucidity makes them present.

In the lucid present I could allow the mother visitations to direct our work, as she had in the acupuncture session, and become more of a facilitator in the encounters, rather than a traditional interpreting therapist. This leap of faith had served me well in my own experiences of the beyond, and I was excited to take the leap in my therapy work.

Making space for the deceased mother gave Dan's non-lucid dreams the feel of the earlier visitations. In one dream he finds his mother in her garden and grows foliage on his body, then embraces her. His mother had loved her garden, and, with her attention, he was thriving.

He dreamed of female horses in the sea. His mother told him to back them out in order that they can see the water. Just as he had benefited from his mother's garden, his female energy, represented by the horses, should keep in touch with the sea. Dan's mother is providing him the nurturance of her garden and the sea, along with the female energy that they both contain.

After sharing the female-horses dream, Dan mentioned that he was in his childhood home for the Fourth of July and saw a doe outside. When he had described his mother as "confused", knocking on the door in his earlier dreams, he said that she looked like a "deer in headlights". We both found it interesting that a female deer appeared after the dream of female horses, and in his mother's garden as well!

What was the therapeutic benefit of Dan's dream encounters with his deceased mother? The feminine touch and energy ended his endless adolescence at midlife, and prompted him to pressure his longtime high-school sweetheart to move to New York and get married. He wanted a home and family of his own.

During this midlife transition he dreamed of his mother in a toll booth that he had to pass through. His attention to her visitations was his payment for access to the road ahead — wife and home. Lucidity enhances attention to the present moment, facilitating the toll booth transaction. Dan paid attention, and the increased energy of lucidity enabled a quantum leap to a life transformation.

Two years after his mother died, Dan dreamed that he was with his family in his childhood home for Easter. He was his current age, while the others were in their teens. The age difference made him lucid in the dream, and everything became "super real". When lucid, Dan asked for his mother, who appears, and the family has a party. "My mother had a lot of fun," he said.

This dream was the highest level of lucidity achieved by Dan, with "super" reality and the ability to summon his mother. Intention was added to the attention that earlier levels of lucidity provided. With intention and attention, lucidity provides even higher transformational energy in therapy.

After two years of increasingly lucid therapy, following his mother's lead, not mine, Dan is his current age in a dream where his family members are teenagers; he has been transformed and is ready for the second half of his life. The two years have convinced me that what I feared were "esoteric dream practices" have a role in my therapy work with those capable of following their dreams and evolving under their guidance.

Dan's proposal of marriage ended their perpetual adolescence and prompted midlife crises for them both. Recently I had a session with Dan in which he told me a dream of going to visit his mother with a friend. I asked why he went, and he said to get her advice.

"What would you ask her?" I continued.

"What to do about my girlfriend." he replied.

"Ask her before you go to sleep tonight," I offered, and he looked reassured. "We'll see what happens."

Dream-incubation questions have been my primary spiritual practice after assisting in my own therapy for many years. I have gotten better responses from dream incubation than from lucidity, so I decided to introduce the technique to Dan.

The next session he shared a dream in which his mother and father are telling him to leave his childhood home.

"It's over," I said. "Your adolescence is over."

Lou Hagood is a licensed psychoanalyst, a member of The National Psychological Association for Psychoanalysts, and practices in New York City. He has led dream-sharing groups at NPAP, The Institute for Noetic Sciences and annual conferences of The International Association for the Study of Dreams, where he has presented papers and led a workshop in dream play. He has published papers on dreams in "The Psychoanalytic Review", and "The Journal of Religion and Health", as well as a book, "Midlife at the Oasis: Dreaming in the Second Half of Life". His current writings on dreams can be found at his blog.

An Extension of Everything Else We Do: Bringing Touch into an Integrated BodyMind Therapy

Claire Haiman

I am a clinical psychologist and a Somatic Experiencing Practitioner with a background in psychodynamic therapy and Dialectical Behavior Therapy. In both psychodynamic therapy and Somatic Experiencing (SE), I began with my own experiences as a client and gradually explored each through professional training, reading, supervision, and practice. The integration of these methods has been, and still is, a journey. As I looked for mentors or teachers in this endeavor, I found little written on the subject and a growing number of clinicians who were grappling with the same questions as me. It seemed we would all build this road by walking.

I started with my own dissertation research, interviewing clinicians who were trained in both psychodynamic and body centered methods about whether, and how, they integrated their work. I wanted to glean an instruction manual of sorts from this project, but instead I found a number of variations in clinicians' approaches. Broadly speaking, they tended to cluster into three groups: people who maintained two different practices, people who continued to practice one method predominantly, sprinkling in some techniques from the other, and people who attempted to synthesize their training. I very much resonated with the impulse to synthesize. I was reluctant to try out various SE techniques in my largely psychodynamic sessions without knowing exactly why I was doing it or what I was aiming for. Some of my peers reported bold interventions and I felt sheepish and overly cautious for hanging back. And yet, I needed to move ahead gradually so that I could take all parts of myself and my training with me, translating them back and forth into a deeply felt model that made sense to me theoretically and experientially.

I entered into the process clinically by bringing greater and greater awareness to physical experiences in session. Using mindfulness and somatic tracking, I observed that my patients were more in touch with what they felt; they could go deeper into their emotions and be guided by sensations, images, and thoughts that would otherwise be overlooked. I also paid attention to my own bodily experience and observed different types of somatic countertransference. In some instances, I would feel what would be termed a congruent countertransference in psychodynamic terms - my throat would tighten or my breath constrict in a way that mirrored the patient's experience.

In others, I would experience a complementary countertransference, where I'd feel the impulse to touch them in a very particular way that seemed to meet a specific need they were experiencing. Long before I physically touched a patient, I experimented with having the patient hold him/herself as well as having us each very consciously put our intention on a particular area and observe what sensations, images, emotions emerged.

Touch - actually putting my hands on a patient - remained something of a bugaboo for me. In part, it was the years of psychodynamic training and the enormous taboo regarding touch: Freud's "slippery slope" that, left unchecked, would lead to exploitation, abuse, the destruction of the treatment. Even though I didn't really believe it, it still had a hold on me. I suppose I was also concerned with litigation issues and malpractice, but that was a more remote fear than the pressing question of technique: how to bring it up? Which patients to approach? Even as I addressed these hurdles and received a general sort of permission from a number of patients to continue with an increased focus on the body that might include touch, I stayed nailed to my chair.

Part of the problem was structural: my office chair was cumbersome; moving it toward a patient was a big production. Once in the chair, it didn't offer a lot of mobility, even if I did move it. And my office was on the small side. There was really no way to include a massage table unless I got rid of my desk and bookshelves. I considered it but realized that I really didn't want that actually, or symbolically: to reject my reading and theory and replace it with touch. I wanted both. I would need a bigger office that could accommodate and represent all parts of me. In the meantime, I got a smaller chair that rolled around and allowed me to move smoothly and sit more upright. And I got another chair for patients: straight-backed and light, it could be moved around easily.

One of the first people I actually touched in session was a patient I'd been working with for years. She has a history of panic disorder and anorexia and tends toward abstinence in most things. She yearns for contact with people but remains guarded and has had few truly intimate relationships. Earlier in our treatment, the somatic work had been around awareness of sensation which led to an observation of being withdrawn into her core so that all the aliveness existed in a thin current along her midline. Extremities were experienced as twisted. Internally there was a sensation of stacking and pulling in opposite directions. She would often sit with her legs crossed, and then crossed again at the ankle. This seemed to capture a deeper sense of being tangled up in herself and also the need to not take up too much space-- an anxiety she clearly acknowledged.

Bringing awareness to this often led to some opening as well as some fear. The benign support of the kidney-adrenal hold (where the therapist places one hand over the patient's kidney - on the back, just below the ribs - and another on the patient's shoulder) appealed as a way of helping her move out of her core and feeling contained to embody herself more fully. However, her counter-dependent stance also made such a hold seem tricky. It was possible that the hold would feel intrusive instead of supportive and she'd withdraw further or brace herself against the contact. Another concern was that she'd feel compelled to "perform" - always an issue with her - and do what she thought I wanted her to do. I also had my own inhibitions about performing, doing it "the right way" and wanting to have it all worked out before I began. This was, after all, uncharted territory for me. To give us both some breathing room, I used an intermediate step of having her imagine being held here, of placing her own hand on her kidney, and tracking sensation; and then of having us both put our intention on that area while she tracked sensation.

The physical touch, when it finally did happen, felt both radical and totally natural. I had observed myself over several sessions experiencing an intense pull to actually touch her. I could imagine exactly where my hand would go and the pressure I would apply. "Oh, I wish I could do a kidney-adrenal hold with her. That's just what she needs," I found myself thinking again and again. It became apparent to me that in my effort to do everything right, to hang back until I figured it all out, I was denying my patient something that I knew she needed. From that perspective, it wasn't ethical to not offer the kidney-adrenal hold. I realized, also that my work was in danger of stagnating. I had been growing in this direction steadily and to not move forward clinically left me with fewer tools at my disposal and less engagement in the here and now of the session.

After discussing the touch I wanted to offer her and getting her permission, I invited her to sit in an upright chair (instead of my couch) and I rolled my chair over. We were so close! It already felt so much more intimate, in ways that were unnerving as well as humanizing. We paused for several moments to explore her experience of my proximity. I looked different, she said - mostly that she wasn't used to seeing me up close, at this angle. We tracked her bodily experience as I sat next to her, with her observing some agitation that then settled down to baseline as this became the new normal. I placed one hand over her kidney. She felt warm and reported an increased sense of grounding as I put my other hand on her shoulder. The warmth expanded through her back and then into her arms. I experienced her as more fully present and bigger than I usually did. She became flushed and I was aware of the heat beneath my hands. She reported feeling a surge of power and heat move through her, as well as some twitching in her arms (both signs of discharge of bound energy).

As the session was ending I slowly retracted my intention and then my hands, while asking her to steadily observe her internal state. She was quiet for several moments and it wasn't clear what she was experiencing. As she opened her eyes, she reported feeling herself withdraw into her core. I offered to move my chair back into its original position (about seven feet from her), wondering if having me so close felt intrusive at this moment. She quickly declined, "No, I want to pull away but I want you to follow me." This perfectly captured a central dynamic in our treatment and in her interpersonal relationships: that she yearned for intimacy and contact while also wanting to flee. And that she wanted to be followed, to be contacted. That piece of it was not so obvious - my own interpretation had been that I was too close, intruding. We imagined together that many people had this response to her, missing altogether the invitation to follow. There was sadness in this and a revelation: she was telling people "you're too close, back off" when she really wanted to be saying, "Come closer, follow me." We were close to the heart of our work.

We reflected on what the experience of me touching her had been like. After talking it through for a while she summed it up, "I thought it would be weird in some way or very different but it ended up feeling natural, like an extension of everything else we do."

That captured my experience as well: after all my apprehensions and hesitations, the touch felt less like a radical departure from some other approach than the logical next step on a steadily negotiated relational experience.

Claire Haiman, Psy.D. is a therapist in private practice in New York City. A clinical psychologist and Somatic Experiencing Practitioner, she has also completed Kathy Kain's Touch Skills Training for Trauma Therapists. Claire works to integrate these methods on a theoretical and practical level with her background in psychodynamic therapy and Dialectical Behavior Therapy. She has much experience working with eating disorders, borderline personality disorder, and other affect regulation problems. Claire's article, "Bridging the Split: Integrating Psychodynamic and Body-Centered Therapies," will be published in the next issue of the International Journal of Body Psychotherapy. She received her doctorate from Rutgers University and did her postdoctoral training at Columbia University.

When Words Were Not Enough

Susan Rudnick

As we sat together in silence, I was struggling, having no words, feeling frustrated and sad, with no seemingly good way to communicate what I wanted to express to C, my client.

This piece is a brief reflection on how I used Focusing to stay connected with myself, navigating my thoughts and feelings as I ended treatment with a client. In particular, when I worked with Focusing, an experiential practice developed by Eugene Gendlin, what unfolded was my, surprising to me, decision to give her a farewell gift. Having initially been trained as a psychoanalyst, where gift giving was not part of the culture, the decision came as a surprise. Reflecting on what went into this decision, I found three powerful streams that guided me: relational and self-psychology, Focusing and implicit intricacy, and a larger perspective that I will call "the more."

I had worked with C. for almost two years by the time she decided to leave NYC and move to the South, where she had a good friend. Leavings are often difficult for me, and this one had a particular poignancy to it. My first sense was, "Oh no, we've just really connected and gotten going", and "there's so much more to do," and along with that came some kind of a knowing that most probably, unlike some other people, once she left, she would not be contacting me in the future. My heart sank.

There was so much more intricacy just in understanding my reactions. C. agreed with me that therapy was valuable to her, but she felt her life in NY was going nowhere, and though moving wouldn't be easy, therapy was not enough to keep her here.

C. had started to see me to work on an abusive relationship with a man she wanted to leave but couldn't. During our time together, she was able to leave him, and we began to learn more about how her childhood, which involved the abuse of major neglect, was impinging on her capacity for creating intimacy in her adult life. However, the traumas of her early life made it very difficult for her to access feelings and thoughts, and we stumbled through a lot of silence and awkwardness, as I attempted to help us find a safe way to work together. I sometimes did a lot of talking, explicating our awkwardness, and appreciating whatever attempts she made to open up.

She had long hair, which she often tied and untied when she felt uncomfortable, and I learned to use that as a cue we needed to change direction. Through it all I felt her struggling along with me with a sense of engagement even though she might not have something to say. She felt most understood at moments when I could say to her that it seemed she had no words, how hard all of this was for her because she couldn't express herself, and how there was so much inside of her that seemed frozen and inaccessible. I realized that my experience of her difficulties expressing herself mirrored my felt sense of our whole process together. I too felt there was so much more that I would want to express and give to her, than I could. I too, felt wordless in the face of her valiant struggle to express herself. Coming up against the vast expanse of her suffering, I admired her grit, and was so rooting for her to find her way. I was also reminded of how I often struggled to understand my developmentally challenged sister, who had difficulty expressing feelings and concepts, but still persevered in her attempts to grow.

So, to let this process go, felt wrenching to me.

Luckily, we had several months to work on this leaving, and during that time there were some shifts that started to help me feel more confident that the work we had done would stay with her and support her life. Somewhere during that time, in the middle of the night I woke up with the thought that I wanted to give her a farewell gift. And I wanted it to be something that she could take with her, a "real" thing.

This felt at first like one of those moments of imagining that I have sometimes, but then don't act on. Coming like that in the depths of the night it would be easy to dismiss as not really credible. I likened it to thinking about an old boy friend, having the thought to "google" him, the next morning, but then, in the light of day, not doing it.

But in this case the thought did not leave me. Something inside me kept listening, and didn't just want to dismiss it. I began to think and struggle with this. At first I thought "No, that's not appropriate." Giving a gift to a patient is something I have hardly ever done (perhaps for a long awaited child that came, or a particular marriage that happened). In the old paradigm psychoanalytic training I received, "real" gifts can be frowned on, and, prior to learning to work in a focusing way, would have been looked upon as a counter -transference reaction that should be analyzed. Since I come from that tradition, and that is part of who I am, it did feel useful to ask the questions from that context: What was my need to give something "concrete"? Why did I need to give something more than the gift of my having been present with her throughout our time together?

I decided to work on these questions over a period of time using Focusing. When I begin this process, I slow down, taking time to bring my attention inside to my chest, abdomen area, just being with whatever is there. I'm asking inside myself, "how am I in this moment? What's the weather like here? How am I in my body about this whole thing of giving a gift?" Then I wait with the attitude of being ready to embrace whatever is coming. As I began to work in this way, I noticed quickly how cramped and tight my body felt. Just in making this decision I noticed that in the previous way I asked these questions, although they were useful, I was seeing this need as pathology. I realized I had been asking from a basic assumption that there must be something wrong with me, and I should find out what neurotic need I would be fulfilling. When I examined myself from the analytic paradigm, which originated in the medical model that looks for symptoms of disease, there was a tendency to become judgmental and critical of myself, which led to a closing off of further exploration. In that paradigm, as well, I would be looking in a quasi-scientific way for an explanation in a cause and effect way for what is causing me to want to give a gift. Thus, for example, I might conclude in a reductionist way that I was overcompensating for a need to fix her, stemming from my childhood compulsion to make my developmentally challenged sister whole again.

When I worked in a focusing way I asked into my felt sense, "What is in me now about all of this now?" I was sensing into the implicit of this whole experience. My experience of this process was one of openness just to what is, without judging it. Here's some of what came. I felt like a mother to her, and mothers give real presents to their children. And then, but she is not my child in that sense, and with that came a kind of sadness and frustration. And then, a sense of how brave and tenacious she has been in her life, and with that the acute awareness of how she's never been given any recognition. And then, a longing in me of how much I really, really, really, want her to know that she is a valuable person, and that I value her. There was also a sensing of her as a little girl and a loving of that in her, and then that there is so much that remains unexpressed between us, and how I want to find a way to do that. Then came a few questions that veered back a little to the older paradigm: "Was I reluctant to let her go? Yes. Was I undervaluing my own impact on her that I need to do this? Maybe. Was I trying to prove something? Not sure what. What does it mean to be a mothering/therapist? Is this a care taking need?" I allowed it all to be there, even the judgments, which all felt a little more spacious.

Each of these had felt sense places that came up for me, and lived in me for a time. The crux of all of this seemed to be about mothering, so I made a big place for the mother in me, and waited. What came was giving and letting go, the sense of giving all I can, and then, as with my own child, having to let her go on her own path. And yes, here too, was an aspect of how I also felt maternal towards my sister.

Then, a larger place emerged for me that I named with the word "limitations." First, the limitations of the therapy process itself, and what we can and cannot do to insure someone's moving forward in their life. Then came the limitation of being human in the face of someone else's suffering. And finally the sentence that came to me was: although words so often clarify and open doors, sometimes words are not enough.

Clearly my struggles as a mother in my personal life, as well as in my work as a therapist are included here, but then something larger emerged. As I stayed with all of this what came for me in a definitive and clear way, was that in giving this gift, something from the deepest part of me that was seeking to be expressed would be coming through to her. This impulse felt like it was arising out of the human condition itself; the experience both of how we are all connected, and how each of us is alone. And how we struggle with all of that. I was now feeling strongly that the gesture of a "real" gift would expand the therapeutic frame, and could be a step that could perhaps allow us to connect in another more basic and rich way. Giving a gift could be a ritual that would honor our time together, carry us through our last session, and perhaps beyond it.

Staying attuned in a focusing way and not closing off that initial impulse supported and nourished a core wellspring place in me. It would have been easy to tune these initial stirrings out, by minimizing their importance, or by reciting chapter and verse of theory I have learned. Listening inside and giving attention to all of that in me allowed me to be true to myself, and understand in a deeper way the wordless intricacy of the therapeutic process, and how I bring myself to it.

More focusing helped me find the gift, which, surprisingly, turned out to be a pair of handmade, curved, beeswax candles that I had originally bought for myself, made in the spiritual community where my sister lived. It felt right to give her something that was mine that I loved, and also reflected a little of my sister's spirit.

Gift in hand, I waited thirty five minutes of the session, had no response to a call, and was ready to leave, when she came rushing in. She had been driving a truck back from a trip to her new city, but told me it felt important for her to come, even though she had been stuck in traffic. She was bursting to tell me that at the very end of the last day of her trip after a series of coincidences, she had found a perfect little house that she could afford to buy, very near where her friend lived. For both of us this felt like such a validation of her move.

When I gave her the gift she giggled like a little girl, and asked if she could unwrap it now. There was a lovely excitement, and a glowing between us. They would go on her new dining room table, she told me. I was feeling that what was being unwrapped and revealed about us encompassed so much more than the act of giving the actual gift. In that moment, I was feeling a sense of awe, and largeness, difficult to describe as anything less than sacred; a moment of sharing, and letting go, and love that bridged the difficulty with words, and, I felt sure, we would both carry in our hearts.

Susan Rudnick LCSW has been in private practice for over thirty years in Manhattan and Westchester. Her special interests include questions of spiritual direction, infertility and adoption, and relationship intimacy issues. She trained analytically at the Karen Horney Institute. Twelve years ago she discovered and fell in love with Focusing. She is a certified Focusing Trainer, and has completed a Focusing based trauma program, led by Shirley Turcotte. She also is part of an ongoing Self Psychology study group. A Zen practitioner, and haiku poet, her chapter, "Coming Home to Wholeness," appears in the book "Into the Mountain Stream: Psychotherapy and Buddhist Experience," ed. Paul Cooper. Susan teaches and supervises for the FORP (Focusing Oriented Relational Psychotherapy) program in New York and South Africa.

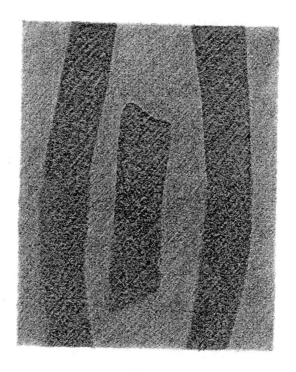

The Consciousness of Babies

Marjorie Rand

I have been a practicing somatic psychotherapist for over 35 years. I was trained in dance/movement, Gestalt, and Neo-Reichian therapies. In practicing Somatic Psychotherapy with adults I became aware that through addressing the body, early pre-verbal memories could be accessed. This knowledge led me to a thorough investigation of object relation theories, particularly those of Winnicott and Kohut, which helped me interpret early life experiences, starting from birth to three years of age. I had no idea that prenatal experiences could also be accessed and I had never heard of the field of Pre and Perinatal Psychology, developed by Thomas Verny, MD. Although I had read about infant mental health, and had followed the work of infant researchers (Beebe, Brazelton, Stern, Tronick, et.al) on videos of experiments with infants and caregivers, I had never seen an actual therapy session with an infant.

Then I observed William Emerson at work. I watched a couple holding their newborn infant in their arms, while Emerson, a pioneer in helping infants resolve birth trauma, sat in front of them. Wordlessly he placed his palms facing the infant about 18 inches away and began moving them around the infant. As he did so, the infant quietly watched him, and after a few moments, the newborn reached out his hand toward William and initiated physical contact with him.

I assumed William was working with the infant's energetic boundaries, staying at the edge until the infant invited him to come closer. At a non verbal level, spatial boundaries define the energy field.

The session proceeded; William scanned the infant's cranium and body for trauma sites associated with the birth process. We know from a fetal perspective that the conjunct points on the fetal cranium and body, particularly neck, shoulders and hips, are where trauma due to a slow birthing progress (stuckness) is likely to occur. When a sensitive area was palpated, the infant reacted emotionally. Remember this is "near touch", not physical touch. The parent's natural inclination was to comfort their baby, but comforting the baby is not necessarily the best response; mirroring the emotion and empathizing with it is more effective. William retreated to the edge of the baby's boundary and waited until the infant reached out once more to engage William. This process continued for the rest of the session; William mirrored the infant's experience and talked to the parents as well.

William called this Birth Re-Facilitation. I was particularly interested in his work with infants who had experienced traumatic births, because the trauma was so close to the surface and not covered up by rigidified defenses, armor, dissociation, etc. I had not seen nor heard of this before. I understood this energetic work with adults, but never even imagined one could work with infants at the very origin of the trauma. Watching William work convinced me that I needed to learn to work this way myself, and I wound up studying with him for nine years and teaching with him for three years.

I also became interested in the work of David Chamberlain, PhD, on prenatal consciousness. I believe it is what we have called cellular consciousness, registered so early that it pervades the whole body and is not connected to cognitive or intellectual consciousness (the body as the "unconscious").

I want to share my amazing emotional experience at this discovery of consciousness in babies and the ability to intervene from the earliest developmental stages throughout the life span. This enabled me to work with the consciousness of the newborn by working with pregnant couples, babies and the prenatal and birth experiences in my adult clients.

Once I observed and learned this work, the ubiquity of birth symbolism and its trauma was impossible to ignore, both in people's language and in their bodies.

I particularly preferred working with couples before conception, or during pregnancy, or after birth in order to make conscious repetitive dysfunctional relational (attachment) issues and release them before the birth of the child. Before neuroscience, we already knew that babies (even unborn babies) had a level of consciousness (cellular), not cognitive, and this is where we can intervene and interrupt these patterns.

We believed that if we could train the parents how to work with the infants energetically, with bonding and mirroring, we could intervene and resolve the early attachment issues from the very start and prevent all kinds of later relational recurring recapitulations of early trauma.

Most parents were really unconscious of the damage and trauma that was being perpetuated upon their newborns in hospital births in the 1980's and 90's. Half of all pregnancies concluded with scheduled C sections; inductions, cord trauma, use of anesthesia and forceps, spinal and epidural anesthesia, premature birth, and the separation of mother and newborn were very common. These parents would not know that they needed to seek treatment, even if they knew it was available.

I went to Switzerland to lead birth training sessions for therapists, and a trainee wanted to bring her 4 year old cesarean born son for a session. He didn't speak English, of course, so the whole session was basically nonverbal. I asked her to bring toys, which children use to communicate; all sessions are client centered, that is, driven by the children. As usual, we started sitting in a circle, a womb circle, and meditated together to create a safe and loving space for the child.   Then the students in training wanted to ask me a question. They wanted to know what a C-section baby would expect or act out. Without thinking, I answered intuitively "rescue fantasy".

The mom and child came in and he unpacked his suitcase full of toys and selected a fire engine and two toy dolls, a boy and a girl, and proceeded to drive the fire engine directly over to me and put up the ladder and send the two dolls up the ladder to safety to me. I have no idea if there was a "lost twin" theme or why there were two dolls, or even if he knew who I was, but he came right to me.

Another child, Alice, had been born blue from oxygen deprivation and had low Apgar scores (a simple test evaluating the health of the newborn), which had caused her to be moved to the NICU (neonatal intensive care unit) where she was subjected to many medical tests which involved a lot of painful heel pricking to get blood for blood work. When she was 15 months old her parents brought her to see me. We had a doll in the office, and, by coincidence, a glass topped table. Alice took the doll to the (cold) glass top table and stuck the heels of the doll, a re-enactment of her own early experience, which was healing in and of itself.

There are many more cases like these where very early separations caused by birth trauma, medical emergencies or hospitalizations of either mother or child or both lie hidden underground, buried beneath some very well developed coping techniques and survival methods that work fine in the world until a crisis like death, divorce, illness, break up, or other loss create a stress too great to contain; then the defenses crumble, revealing the tiny emergent self that had been abandoned long ago.

Sometimes people with these kinds of buried experiences decide to seek treatment when they are adults. One such person is Linda, a sixtyish Gay woman who had been in a relationship with her live-in partner Barbara for 18 years. The past several years had been rocky--Barbara was cheating on Linda and lying about it; ultimately, Barbara moved out.

Linda had a good paying job and was a highly developed woman with many friends, but she was completely devastated and betrayed by the breakup of her relationship with Barbara, and fell into a deep depression, barely functioning, and obsessed about Barbara all the time. She felt that with Barbara's departure she would not survive, that she had lost part of herself. In fact Linda had given part of herself up to sustain the relationship with Barbara.

Linda had an uneventful childhood, raised in a middle class, loving environment with little obvious trauma on the surface to explain how she had fallen into such a deeply painful regressed place. It was necessary to go very far back to the earliest developmental stage to find the clue.

At the time of Linda's birth, Linda's mother was suffering with pneumonia and her life was in jeopardy. Linda was not allowed to be held by her or even seen by her for several weeks, until her mother recovered.

The good and the not so good of it was that her grandmother was able to care for her during that very important stage of attachment--the bonding stage, Good because Linda had already begun to attach to her grandmother in utero, not so good because Linda was not allowed to bond during the critical stage with her biological mother (an abandonment almost like an adoption).

While uncovering that incident was not enough in and of itself to completely relieve the symptoms of the grown Linda, it did reveal the origin of the injury and start the healing process of the newborn Linda.

Recently I was working with a woman on pelvic pain issues and in asking about the birth of her children (both C sections), I learned that her son is very aggressive and loves to wrestle and play physical games. I interpreted this as his attempts to resolve his C section issues; and this alone changed their relational dynamic. I now have him doing handstands against the wall as therapy.

I do want to make clear that my particular way of working is an integration of my Integrative Body Psychotherapy (IBP) work, Yoga therapy, developmental movement re-patterning and all the many things I have studied and integrated over the years. My work is a containment and resource model, so trauma is not re-lived and old patterns are not strengthened, but new neural pathways are laid down by new movement patterns which integrate the body/mind.

I value presence and somatic empathy as my therapeutic contribution in the session. I mirror what I see, sense and hear, more often hearing the music than the words. I accompany my clients on a journey to an unknown place; I do not lead them there. Most often we use breath to clear the mind and open the body and bring awareness to a state of mindfulness of the present.

Usually though, we do not set out to do a "birth" session. The material just comes up and skips around from early to later developmental stages, as you will see from the following transcript of an IBP session.

Colette began the session by scanning her body and reporting her awareness. Spontaneous imagery emerged from body to mind, not mind to body. This imagery represented both her own stuckness in the birth canal and subsequent delivery by Cesarean section.

When birth images emerge from a holding pattern in the pelvic segment, later traumas to the pelvis can also be released. In Colette's case the first memory was of a fibroid tumor being removed from her uterus, which she compared to giving birth by Cesarean section. This led to a memory of an abortion.

Finally, the memory of the abortion allowed her to come to some acceptance of her relationship with her mother, which allowed her to begin some inner healing. The therapist did not touch her during the session, although Colette was instructed to perform self-release techniques, such as massaging her belly.

As you will see, constantly referring Colette back to her body, where the awareness arose, contributed to the depth and resolution of this session.

T: What are you aware of in your body?
C: I feel a sensation in my abdomen.
T: Can you describe it?
C: It is a dark space.
T: Stay with the awareness and tell me what happens in your body.
C: It seems like a room, a large room, and it's locked.
T: Describe the body feeling of the room being locked.
C: It feels so stuck. It's very tight there and it's growing.
T: The space in your abdomen is like a large locked room and it's growing.
C: Yes and now nothing is happening.
T: Stuck and nothing happening.
C: Oh my God!!
T: What are you aware of now?
C: I'm aware of a circle, a sphere.
T: Where is that in your body?

C: It's hard for me to put my awareness there because I'm numb there from surgery. I had a large fibroid tumor removed in 1990.

T: *Put your hand on that area and massage it.*

C: I gave birth in that surgery to a very large tumor and it was a cesarean.

T: *Keep massaging it.*

C: I can always feel pain; you know that line between numbness and pain.

T: *Pain is feeling.*

C: Don't you think having a growth there has to do with old stuff?

T: *It sounds like it could have a relationship to your own birth.*

C: (Starts to cry.)

T: *What is happening?*

C: I'm remembering the abortion I had that has never been processed. I feel guilt.

T: *Where in your body do you feel that?*

C: The pain isn't there anymore. I keep going to that spot inside my uterus where life began and life ended.

T: *Stay with your awareness of that spot.*

C: I could not have a child because of my fear that I would bring a child up the way I was brought up. I had the abortion after my mother had just died. I drove myself there by myself; I drove myself home by myself. I had no support.

T: *When your mother died, you had to give up hope that your relationship with her would ever be healed.*

C: Immediately my back went out. Crying out for support and attention, I was flat on my back for five weeks. So, I processed it in an aborted way (begins to laugh)... (Silence for a moment.)

C: I'm remembering when my mother died and I had a vision in which she came to me and kissed me goodbye, and I never saw her again. She left. There was no way for her to help me when she was on the earth or when she departed.

T: *What are you feeling?*

C: (Silent)

T: *What is going on?*

C: I had no idea this stuff was still there. I'm not angry at all. I have to stop treating myself the way my mother treated me.

We cannot recover these experiences only through taking a history, although most therapists who do not concern themselves with body issues rarely ask about a client's birth. They have to be re-experienced and released on an emotional/energetic level in the body (where they were first experienced). However, they are not meant to be re-lived and thereby re-traumatizing, but witnessed in the empathic presence of the therapist who functions as the safe container for the experience until the client can integrate the ability to create an empathic relationship with his injured sense of self. I typically begin treatment with the following intake form, asking specific questions.

- Was your pregnancy planned?
- Were you a wanted child?
- Were you premature?

- Were you in an incubator? For how long?
- Was your birth difficult?
- Was your mother in poor physical or emotional
health during her pregnancy with you?
- Did she experience any losses or dramatic events
during her pregnancy with you?
- Were there any miscarriages, still births or abortion
prior to your birth?
- Did your parent(s) want a child of the opposite
gender?
- Were you adopted?
- As an infant were you separated from your mother at
birth?
- Did you have any medical problems or early
hospitalizations?

I cannot emphasize enough how understanding the significance and power of these early experiences has changed my entire outlook on how I perceive clients and how I do therapy with them. Just inquiring about their birth cuts through months of therapy. I have a new appreciation of how addictions are formed for instance (anesthesia during birth). But mainly, I value the ability to work with pregnant couples and new parents to alleviate the trauma before it sets in as a life long pattern.

Marjorie L. Rand, Ph.D. has been a psychotherapist and Master Trainer for 36 years. She specializes in Integrative Body Psychotherapy, Dance/Movement therapy, Supported Yoga Therapy and meditation. She is in Private practice in Los Angeles, CA. She has trained psychotherapists throughout Europe, Canada, Israel and the US. She is the co-author of 3 books- Body, Self and Soul *with Jack Rosenberg (1985),* Getting In Touch, *edited by Christine Caldwell (1997), and* Helping The Helper *with Babette Rothschild (2004) and many published articles. She is a founding member of USABP, and is presently a peer reviewer for the new IJBP.*

Room to Grow

Robin Kappy

"No man [or woman] can tell what the future may bring forth, and small opportunities are often the beginning of great enterprises." - Demosthenes

I was smaller than my siblings. I mean, as a person. That was my experience for at least the first half of my life. They are 6 and 8 years older than I and have enjoyed full lives, while I grew used to measuring my successes on a minuscule scale. My "big" sister is actually several inches shorter than I am; I never would have noticed if not for the help of a dear friend. My brother was in the middle, and though he was a few inches taller, it would be years before I experienced myself as significant enough to see eye to eye.

With buried wishes of starting a private practice, upon graduation from social work school in 1991, still feeling painfully small, I began work at a settlement house founded for immigrants at the turn of the century. I felt like a sort of immigrant myself, in my little office, with people who came to feel like family, just a few blocks from home. I became part of the place and did not think I would ever leave the security of the "settlement" house.

Encouraged by referrals, in evenings after work, I started a private psychotherapy practice in a "spare" room in my tiny-as-could be third floor walk-up in bohemian Greenwich Village. Being the tag-along "caboose" in my family, I was used to living in limited physical and psychic quarters. I could not picture myself as having any of the "more" I saw my colleagues enjoying. I accepted low fees and expectations, and those willing to walk up the stairs. Anyone requiring the luxury of an elevator and a waiting room went elsewhere. After a number of years, as my clientele grew, feeling as if I was risking what little I had, I went out on my own into full-time private practice.

There was something delightfully insular about the place. However, wanting my long-time partner to move in with me, and needing to reassign that tiny bit of a room I called my office; I hesitatingly moved my practice to a place with even less square footage, on nearby East 11th Street. I assumed "small" was all that was meant for me as a therapist and, though I still had no waiting room, the office building had elevators, was affordable, and suited me well enough.

During the ten years I spent in my "mini-office" on 11th, I became a supervisor and faculty member in the Focusing Oriented Relational Psychotherapy Program, an EMDR practitioner, and found a way to weave focusing with that powerful modality. My love for my work and confidence as a psychotherapist snuck up on me as I gained years of experience and contact with an extraordinary group of colleagues. Also during this time, after thirty years in my very humble home, my partner and I received an offer we could not refuse and moved to a larger apartment. As I reflect now, it was as if the physical space around me was growing to accommodate an expanding sense of myself.

In a seemingly parallel universe, I had the "small opportunity" to begin taking art classes and immediately became intimately involved with learning to draw realistically from life. Just as I am when at work in my office, I was very focused, now on a serious quest to develop my drawing skills. However, right from the start, what I learned went far beyond the easel. I took each lesson as a lesson in life:

Lesson Number One:

Draw what you see, not what you think you see. Make no misguided assumptions. Observe and experience the myriad of nuances and gestures of every shape and form. *Psychotherapeutic Translation:* Listen fully, there is much more to hear and experience than what at first seems apparent.

Lesson Number Two:

To clearly represent whole shapes and forms on paper, one must see and understand broad and subtle angles and relationships. *Psychotherapeutic Translation:* When fully listening to the whole person, subtle relationships and meanings reveal themselves.

Lesson Number Three:

Variously named types of darks and lights describe each object and subject. Understand how they interplay beautifully and represent these observations with a pencil. *Psychotherapeutic Translation:* Each person has light and dark aspects, and is wholly beautiful. Hold a sense of the wholeness. Reflect well.

Lesson Number Four:

Practice. *Psychotherapeutic Translation:* Practice.

In classrooms past, I had been distressed by a perpetual sense of inferiority. With my drawing pad and pencils, I found a persistence in myself I had not seen since social work school. There, in compensation, I was pointedly determined to be a good student. Now drawing, I did not want to stop. As my drawing skills increased, so did my sense of confidence at the easel, and in myself. I developed a daily practice, and my daily practice developed me.

I was gaining ground on understanding creative process, and drew parallels between the skills of observation and listening. I came to consider each lesson and aspect of my creative life to be in service of my growth as a person and therapist. For a short while, I found it difficult to switch back and forth between my passions, as if two separate parts of my brain were required to be a therapist and an artist. With the invaluable love and support of very important people in my life, I gradually integrated my two identities into a new sense of personal and professional wholeness and magnitude.

Increasingly, though I tried hard to ignore it, I felt my meager office constricting my ability to blossom. Against any and all of my previous expectations, I began to dream of having a larger office with a waiting room. My dear friend and colleague wanted to move her office too and as we took to visualizing and strategizing together, I quaked in my too-small boots. When she found a building we might move to, a dogged fear of moving beyond the security, familiarity and smallness of my office kept my hopes at bay. During the next year, I vacillated between a sometimes still painful personal and archaic sense of limitation and inadequacy and a deepening desire for something more, something larger.

Then we were offered a space that was just right for us in every way. I was scared! Signing the new lease and giving notice felt like jumping off a very high diving board and trusting the water below to receive me. And yet, I jumped. My fear became exhilaration: inner and outer space was expanding, and I prepared to move.

I let go of many things before moving: old files, books, pictures and things that no longer represent me, wanting openness for my new beginning. I carefully chose soothing colors for our new walls and beautiful furnishings, and set a calm, open tone. After the move, I started seeing clients as soon as I could. I now often linger here for whole hours at the end of the day, reflecting upon how at home I am in these rooms, as though they had been waiting for me.

As I listen for my next client to enter the waiting room, I am running my hand along the edge of the soft, reassuring, richly colored wood and having a look around. Not only do I have more space and a waiting room, I am surprised to discover that I am now a bigger person...with room to grow.

Robin Kappy, LCSW is a certified Focusing Oriented Psychotherapist and supervisor. A skillful and empathic psychotherapist with years of professional experience, her specialties include the treatment of recent and early-childhood trauma, issues of creativity, depression, anxiety, relationships and sleep-related problems. She is a certified EMDR practitioner and faculty member and supervisor for the Focusing Oriented Relational Psychotherapy Program. She and Susan Rudnick, LCSW cofounded Flatiron Psychotherapy Associates and offer "Rest Well Tonight," a focusing-oriented approach to assisting people who experience difficulties falling or staying asleep, or wake feeling un-rested. In addition to a passionate engagement with her work as a psychotherapist, Robin loves to draw and paint. Her drawings and paintings have appeared in a number of venues. She writes about the integration of psychotherapy, creativity and the topic of beauty on her blog: Stepping Through Beauty.

The 10 illustrations between chapters are drawings by Robin Kappy.

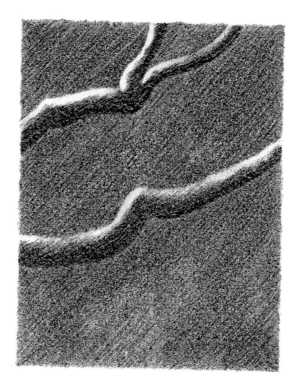

The One Word We Knew

Marianne Gunther

It was my first day on the hospice unit and I was nervous. I wasn't sure how I could offer art therapy to individuals in the final stages of their life. I had completed the required hospice training, understood that listening and being an empathic presence was essential, but, being a creative person, it didn't feel like enough, I had to do something.

So I brought my pencils and sketch pad and decided to offer to draw portraits. This sketch is one of the very first faces I drew. The nurses on the unit asked me to sit with *Abuela*, their nickname for her, as her family members had not yet arrived for their evening visit, and it seemed she could use some company.

What they didn't tell me was that she spoke only Spanish, a language I regrettably never studied.

When I arrived she greeted me with a warm smile and a rush of Spanish. I responded with the only Spanish I knew; Hola/Hello and Si/Yes. She proceeded to talk, assuming I knew what she was saying.

I showed her my pencils and pad and gestured my intent to draw her face. She smiled, nodded and said, "Si, Si." "Si" I said proceeded to sit near her bed and began to draw. She began to talk and talk and talk! I listened and heard the familiar cadence of storytelling. Somehow, I knew when to validate her, at various points in her monolog with a simple "Si." Despite the language barrier I watched her begin to settle down, her speech sounded less agitated, and her words began to slow down and eventually she became quiet. I showed her my drawing. She took hold of my hand and smiled.

"Si" she said. "Si" I said. The one word we knew and the only word we needed.

Marianne Gunther is a New York State- licensed creative art psychotherapist in private practice in New York City. She is a bereavement group facilitator at A Caring Hand: The Billy Esposito Foundation; *has consulted for* Art & Soul ™, *MJHS Hospice & Palliative and* Continuum Hospice Care. At Continuum, *she established the* Portrait Project, *supervising volunteer artists in offering portraiture as a therapeutic intervention, and was website moderator for the* Art Therapy Forum for the Grieving Center, *winner of the 2007 W3 Silver Award by the International Academy of Visual Arts. Marianne received her B.F.A. from the School of the Museum of Fine Arts, Tufts University, Boston, her Masters in art therapy from Pratt Institute and is currently studying with the Institute for Expressive Analysis, NY. Graduate of the Emma Willard School, in 1999, she was awarded Outstanding Young Alumna award, in recognition of her achievements in creative art psychotherapy.*

The drawing described in this story is on the following page.

Afterword:
A Process of Relational Mindfulness

Serge Prengel

What happens when people are mindfully engaged in a relational process? They are affected by it.

That psychotherapy has the power to change clients is basic to the "talking cure". But, for a long time, it was considered just as basic that the therapist was not affected by this process.

Of course, it was deemed absolutely necessary that analysts have their own analysis, i.e. that they be changed by the process. But the idea was that they would reach a point where they could be neutral in their clients' process.

Of course, Freud himself kept evolving his theory of what it is to be human as he kept learning from his interactions with his clients. But he would not have described his evolving narrative of the human psyche as a journey of personal transformation. He saw it as scientific observation similar to what other scientists were doing in other fields.

What has changed in more recent times is the sense that therapy is an intersubjective experience: It is not just that interacting with a client happens to affect the therapist; it is actually very much part of what makes therapy work.

There is a parallel process going on. On the one hand, the therapist is tracking the client, which, for many of us these days is not just about words, or content, but also involves attention to felt sense, movement and body language. On the other hand, we are also tracking ourselves: Our felt sense of the experience, how we resonate, or are otherwise affected by the client.

This is a mindful process, contemplative but not passive at all. Moment by moment, the therapist is making micro-assessments and micro-decisions, paying attention to what happens with the client, as well as paying attention to what happens inside. This could be described as "applied phenomenology": Each micro decision influences what happens next.

This is an active process, where our attention is fully engaged. But it is not the kind of hyper-vigilant attention that occurs when our sympathetic nervous system is engaged. The pressure of imminent danger brings out knee-jerk reactions that are based on instinct, or fear conditioning. In this mindful space, we have room to go beyond reactivity. We can effectively face the situation as it is, and be responsive to it.

It is not always easy for therapists to do this, nor do we always do it well. We are not striving for perfection. Our intent is on mindfulness. Our attitude imparts a certain quality of roominess to the interaction, making it easier for clients to enter a mindful space. A space where change is possible.

As we live and breathe in this space, we too are affected. Through the phenomenological interactions of therapy, we pursue a background dialogue with our "model of mind". This is not just an abstract construction about this specific client, or the human mind in general... It is also very much about "who I am".

To put it more simply: As we are immersed in the process of therapy, we are very much in process. Hence the "defining moments" that we experience in our work.

And, as we inhabit a space where it is possible for us to change, we contribute to making it a space where clients can change.

We are inviting you to continue exploring this process with us on Linked In:

http://linkedin.integrativeprocess.com

Biographies

Each chapter is followed by the bio of its author. Information about the artwork is on next page.

The editors of this book are Serge Prengel and Lynn Somerstein.

Serge Prengel, LMHC, is in private practice in New York City. He sees change as a creative process, driven by the depth and immediacy of felt-sense experience. He wrote Scissors: A Whimsical Fable About Empowerment *as well as other books, and is the editor of* Somatic Perspectives on Psychotherapy. *He has also been leading experiential workshops in a variety of venues.*

Lynn Somerstein, PhD, NCPsyA, LP, RYT, licensed psychoanalyst in private practice, is Executive Director of the Institute for Expressive Analysis. Dr. Somerstein is on the editorial board of the Psychoanalytic Review and the author of numerous articles about yoga, anxiety, attachment issues and psychotherapy. Dr. Somerstein is also an international speaker, and has presented her work in India, Turkey, China, and in the United States. She uses the wisdom she has gained as a yoga teacher, psychologist and student of Ayurveda, or Indian life knowledge, to help people reach their innermost goals.

Artwork:

The 10 drawings between chapters are by Robin
Kappy, who also wrote a chapter. See her bio at the
end of that chapter, Room to Grow.

The drawing that follows Marianne Gunther's
story, The One Word We Knew, is by her.

The cover art is by Cathy Marie Begg. She says:
"This picture, for me, is a woman reflecting upon her
life as she comes to meet the current moment of her
life."

Her bio: *Parent, Artist, Educator and Therapist, all
interactive callings. I have viewed the world through the eyes
of an artist for as long as I can remember. Though growing
up with two military parents presented a practical
framework for career choices. This led me to the field of
Education and a Masters in Counseling. However, my art
remained close at hand. Growing up in San Diego and being
imported to NJ as a teen offered a wide variety for
interpreting life. My artwork has often been described as
work in movement. Using pen and ink, and in recent years
wood carving or sawdust relief, I attempt to couple
emotional connections from my life and community. My
artwork resides in homes in the United States, as well as
other countries. My current studio and gallery (Canal 43) is
located in New Hope Pa.*